# TROPICAL PUNCH

## quilt designs with a florida flavor

That Patchwork Place®

## marilyn dorwart

## Acknowledgments

Thanks to Barbara Kern and Judy O'Donnell for proofing every word and number. They truly made sense and sentences out of all my words.

Thanks to Merrilyn Heazelwood, author of *Cottage Garden,* for allowing me to use her iris and hollyhocks.

Thanks to Suzy Komara, for stitching so many of the silk flowers.

Thanks to Charity Burton for her able assistance making "Flamingo à la Andy."

Thanks to all my friends and family; you have been so very supportive.

Special thanks to my husband, Bill, who has encouraged me at every turn of my quilting career. There would be no Quilters Marketplace, nor this book, without him. Now I am trying to get him to let me put the kitchen in a garage sale. Maybe one day.

### MISSION STATEMENT

*WE ARE DEDICATED TO PROVIDING QUALITY PRODUCTS AND SERVICE BY WORKING TOGETHER TO INSPIRE CREATIVITY AND TO ENRICH THE LIVES WE TOUCH.*

**Library of Congress Cataloging-in-Publication Data**

Dorwart, Marilyn,
    Tropical punch : quilt designs with a Florida flavor / Marilyn Dorwart.
      p.   cm.
    ISBN 1-56477-133-4
  1. Appliqué—Patterns. 2. Quilting—Patterns. 3. Patchwork—Patterns. 4. Florida in art. I Title.
TT779. D67  1997                97-12666
746.46'041—dc21                    CIP

## Credits

Editor-in-Chief . . . . . . . . . . . . . . . . . . . . Kerry I. Smith
Technical Editor . . . . . . . . . . . . . . . . . . Janet White
Managing Editor . . . . . . . . . . . . . . . . . . . Judy Petry
Copy Editor . . . . . . . . . . . . . . . . . . . . . . Tina Cook
Proofreader . . . . . . . . . . . . . . . . . . . . . Leslie Phillips
Design Director . . . . . . . . . . . . . . . Cheryl Stevenson
Cover Designer . . . . . . . . . . . . . . . . . Amy Shayne
Text Designer . . . . . . . . . . . . . . . . . . . . . Kay Green
Production Assistant . . . . . . . . . . Claudia L'Heureux
Illustrator . . . . . . . . . . . . . . . . . . . . . . Robin Strobel
Illustration Assistant . . . . . . . . . . Mary Ellen Buteau
Photographer . . . . . . . . . . . . . . . . . . . . Brent Kane

Tropical Punch: Quilt Designs with a Florida Flavor ©1997 by Marilyn Dorwart

That Patchwork Place, Inc., PO Box 118
Bothell, WA 98041-0118 USA

Printed in Hong Kong
02 01 00 99 98 97     6 5 4 3 2 1

17.95

# TABLE OF CONTENTS

# INTRODUCTION

The art of appliqué is alive and well in the world of quilting. When this book began to form in my mind, I knew it would showcase preassembled-appliqué techniques, which I developed while making "Americana in Appliqué" (shown below), the Florida winner for the 1986 Great American Quilt Contest. I used the preassembled-appliqué process for most of the blocks, but I found it most valuable in the U.S. Capitol block. I reverse-appliquéd the windows on each section of the building, appliquéd the building sections to each other, and then appliquéd the completed building to the background.

A variety of projects will inspire you to try the two appliqué techniques I present in this book. Some of the quilts look complicated, but they are quite easy when you know the construction secrets. Step-by-step directions take you through the appliqué. There are no mysteries in these pages.

My love of embroidery adds an additional element to my quilts. When I appliqué, it just seems natural to add embroidered details. It was especially fun to design "The Market-place," shown on page 18. It looks difficult to make all those beautiful flowers, but again, it's all in knowing how. I used only four embroidery stitches in the whole piece. What could be easier?

Just to prove that I do own and use a sewing machine, I designed a quilt called "Flamingo à la Andy," shown on page 19. I always thought Andy Warhol's works were such fun, and they were the inspiration for this wall hanging, with just a hint of Art Deco thrown in.

In the 1930s Art Deco was the rage, and it's making a comeback in the 1990s. Many people collect Deco-style furniture, art, and jewelry. Art Deco buildings can be seen across the country, but nowhere are there as many in one place as South Beach in Florida. It was fun to add a spark of Art Deco to some of my quilts.

Have fun creating your own versions of these projects, or make them just as they are shown. I hope the quilts are unusual and challenging enough to stimulate the experienced quilter, simple and clever enough to entice the novice.

## AMERICANA IN APPLIQUÉ

By Marilyn Dorwart, 1986,
Delray Beach, Florida, 72" x 72".
Florida winner of the Great American
Quilt Contest, 1986.

# GENERAL QUILTMAKING

Use 100% cotton fabric. Prewash, treat with spray starch, and press all fabrics before starting a project. The spray starch makes the fabric crisp and manageable.

Read through the directions before beginning a project. Pressing between each step will increase your piecing accuracy.

## SUPPLIES

**Each quilt project requires the following tools and materials.**
Basting needles, curved or darning
Batting
Pins
Quilting needles and thread
Rotary cutter
Rotary mat
Rotary ruler
Sewing threads to match the project
Sharp scissors
Spray starch

**Appliqué projects require a few more supplies.**
¾"-long appliqué pins
Appliqué needles
Gluestick
Scissors sharp enough to cut to a point
Template material
Threads to match appliqué fabrics

## FABRIC SELECTION

Selecting fabric for an appliqué quilt can be an adventure. Look for the color you want, and then look at the scale of the print. Don't be afraid of large-scale prints. Try to look beyond the overall pattern of the fabric to see the distinct parts you can use in different areas of your quilt.

Take a window template when you go fabric shopping (see below), or use one as you examine fabrics from your stash. Move the window around on fabrics to locate areas that might look best as appliqué pieces—you might find flower petals lurking in a cowboy print.

For an appliqué flower made of several fabrics, choose several different prints in various shades of the same color. Imagine a light source shining on the quilt, making the tops of the flowers lighter and the undersides darker. Choose different values of the flower color to create this illusion.

Try colors and patterns you've never used before. You may be pleasantly surprised by the results.

### Making a Window Template

*Trace an appliqué pattern onto Mylar or stiff paper. Carefully cut on the drawn lines.*

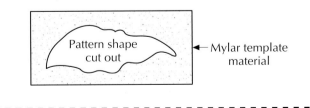

Pattern shape cut out — Mylar template material

## PREASSEMBLED APPLIQUÉ

It's often easiest to assemble appliqué motifs that have two or more pieces *before* you appliqué them to the background. Instead of worrying about whether you can get the pieces of a bird to fit together properly *and* cover placement marks on the fabric background, you simply appliqué the pieces together and then place the entire bird on the background. Once you get used to using preassembled-appliqué techniques, you'll no longer need to trace appliqué pattern lines onto the background fabric for placement.

Technique 1 works best for patterns in which each appliqué overlaps only one other piece. The main piece is not cut out until all other pieces are appliquéd to it. The sandpipers in "Definitely Deco," shown on page 17, are good examples. You appliqué the cap and wing to the body and then cut out the entire sandpiper. Technique 2 is best for patterns with multiple layers, such as the lilies and tulips in the flower quilts and the sea shells in "Definitely Deco." For either method, follow these important steps.

1. Because appliqué shrinks the background slightly, cut the background pieces larger than the finished size, and then trim them after all the appliqué is complete. Trimming to size also enables you to cut away frayed edges.
2. To make templates, trace the appliqué patterns onto a sheet of Mylar. Make small markings where pieces overlap. (I refer to these markings as joining marks. They are indicated on the appliqué patterns with arrows.) Write the number of the pattern piece, which indicates the piecing sequence, on the template.
3. Cut out the templates exactly on the drawn line.
4. Using an emery board, sand the edges of the plastic templates so that you can trace around them smoothly.
5. Trace around each template, onto the right side of the appropriate appliqué fabric. Transfer the joining marks to the fabric, just outside the drawn line.

   Continue with the instructions for Technique 1 or 2, whichever is best suited to your project.

## Technique 1

1. Trace template 1, the main appliqué piece (the one that will lie under the others), onto the right side of the appropriate fabric, adding the joining marks. *Do not cut out piece 1.* If the pattern requires more than one of that piece, trace it as many times as necessary, but be sure to leave enough room between the tracings for the other appliqué pieces to be added. In "Definitely Deco," for example, you need several sandpipers, so you would trace each body onto the fabric, leaving enough room to add the wing and cap.
2. Trace piece 2, with joining marks, onto the correct fabric. Cut out piece 2, adding a ⅛"-wide seam allowance.
3. Place piece 2 on top of the tracing of piece 1, aligning the joining marks. Appliqué piece 2 to piece 1. Repeat with any other piece that lies on piece 1.
4. Cut around piece 1, adding a ⅛"-wide seam allowance, and carefully trim the fabric under the pieces appliquéd to piece 1.
5. Appliqué the completed unit to the background.

## Technique 2

1. Trace template 1, with joining marks, onto the right side of the appropriate fabric. Cut out the piece, adding a seam allowance that is at least ½" wide.
2. Trace template 2, with joining marks, onto the correct fabric. Cut out the piece, adding a ⅛"-wide seam allowance. (If piece 2 will be overlapped by another appliqué piece, add a ½"-wide seam allowance.) Align the joining marks, and appliqué piece 2 to piece 1, stitching between the joining marks. Begin and end with a secure knot.

3. Trim the seam allowance of the appliqué unit to ⅛". Appliqué the unit to the background.

Larger seam allowance on edges where additional pieces will be appliquéd

Continue adding petals to the unit as for piece 2.

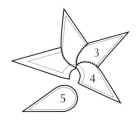

Cut out the final piece for the unit, adding a ⅛"-wide seam allowance.

## Needle-Turn Appliqué

This stitching method works better than any other for preassembled units. Use Sharps or Appliqué needles, which are long and slender, and appliqué thread, which is thinner than regular sewing thread. Use machine-embroidery thread if you cannot find appliqué thread.

1. Pin or baste the appliqué in place. Thread the needle with a single strand of thread, making a knot at one end. Bring the needle and thread up through the background at the edge of the appliqué.

2. Hold the appliqué with your nonsewing hand, thumb on top near the marked turning line. Use the point of the needle to turn under the seam allowance so that the folded edge is just inside the drawn line. Turn under 1 or 2 stitch lengths at a time. Just before bringing the needle up, pull the folded edge back slightly with your thumb to expose the tiniest bit of the seam allowance. Bring the needle and thread up through the fabric a thread from the edge, and pull gently. When released, the turned edge will fall back over the stitch, rendering it invisible.

## Making Perfect Points

1. Trim the seam allowance at the point as shown.
2. Appliqué almost to the point.
3. To reduce bulk at the point, lift the appliqué piece and trim a little more of the seam allowance underneath the appliquéd side.
4. Fold the seam allowance under at the point, make a stitch at the point, and then fold the other side under to form the point.

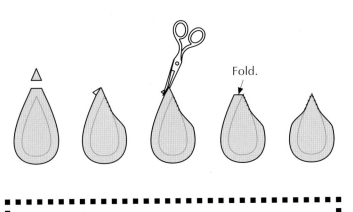

Fold.

## Tip

*If an appliqué piece begins to fray, draw your needle across a fabric gluestick, lightly coating the needle with glue. Rub the coated needle along the edge of the seam allowance and press the piece to the background, temporarily basting the seam allowance and frays in place.*

## Clipping Points and Curves

I clip points and curves only if the appliqué fabric will not follow a graceful curve or make a sharp V. Clip once for a V, several times for a curve. Reinforce a V by making a couple small stitches on each side of the bottom point to firmly hold the tiny seam allowance.

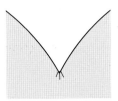

# EMBROIDERY

■ ■ ■ ■ ■ ■ ■ ■ ■ ■ ■ ■ ■ ■ ■

## Silk-Ribbon Embroidery

Use no more than a 12" to 15" length of ribbon for embroidery, or the ribbon will fray. Keep the ribbon as flat as possible against the background to allow its beauty to show.

Start with a knot at one end of the ribbon. To finish a stitch, bring the ribbon to the back and lay it across the nearest stitch. Using a small needle and regular thread, sew the ribbons together with an overcasting stitch. Cut the thread and ribbon, leaving a short tail on each of them.

The silk-ribbon stitch shown below must be done with ribbon, all the other stitches can be done either with ribbon or with embroidery floss.

## Embroidery Stitches

Silk-ribbon stitch

Stem stitch

French knot

Lazy daisy stitch

Satin stitch

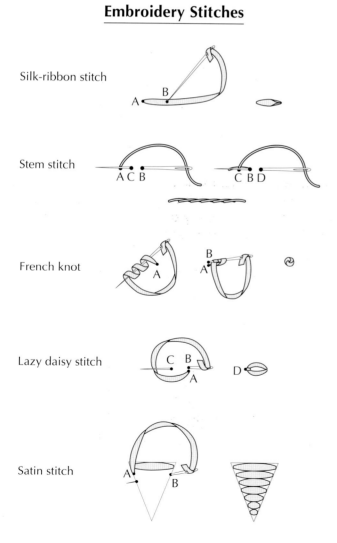

# BORDERS

■ ■ ■ ■ ■ ■ ■ ■ ■ ■ ■ ■ ■ ■

## Borders with Straight-Cut Corners

1. Measure the length of the quilt top down the center. Cut border strips to that measurement.
2. Mark the centers of the quilt top and the border strips. Pin the borders to the sides of the quilt top, matching the center marks and ends and easing as necessary. Sew the border strips in place. Press the seams toward the border.
3. Measure the width of the quilt through the center, including the side borders just added. Cut border strips to that measurement, piecing as necessary. Mark the center of the quilt top and the border strips. Pin the borders to the sides of the quilt top, matching the center marks and ends and easing as necessary. Sew the border strips in place. Press the seams toward the border.

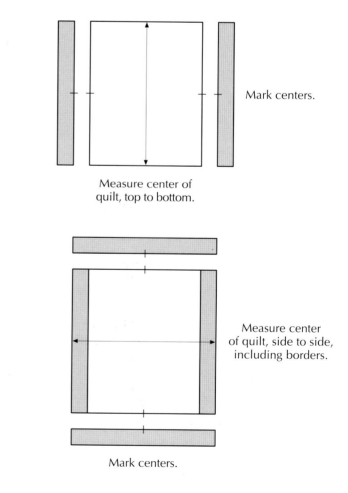

Mark centers.

Measure center of quilt, top to bottom.

Measure center of quilt, side to side, including borders.

Mark centers.

## Borders with Mitered Corners

1. Estimate the finished width and length of your quilt, including borders. Cut border strips to this length plus 2" to 3" more. If your quilt has multiple borders, sew the individual strips together and treat the resulting unit as a single strip. Joined strips make mitering the corners easier and more accurate.

2. In the seam allowance of the quilt top, mark the seam intersections at the corners, and mark the center of each edge. On each border strip, mark the finished endpoints of the border. Using a ¼"-wide seam allowance, stitch the borders to the quilt, matching the centers and end marks. The border strip should extend the same distance beyond the quilt top at each end. Start and stop your stitching ¼" from the corners of the quilt; press the seams toward the borders.

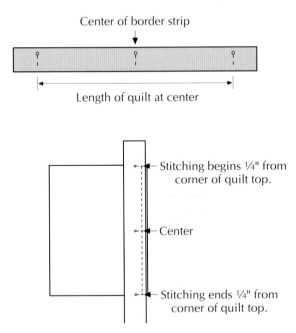

Center of border strip

Length of quilt at center

Stitching begins ¼" from corner of quilt top.

Center

Stitching ends ¼" from corner of quilt top.

3. Lay the first corner to be mitered on an ironing board. Fold one strip under at a 45° angle, adjusting so seam lines match perfectly. Press and pin.

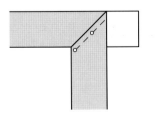

Fold border strip under at a 45° angle and pin.

4. Fold the quilt, right sides together, lining up the edges of the border. If necessary, draw a pencil line on the crease, using a ruler, to make the line more visible. Stitch on the pressed crease, sewing from the corner to the outside edge.

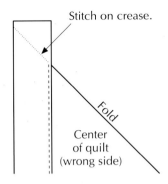

Stitch on crease.

Fold

Center of quilt (wrong side)

5. Press the seam open and trim excess from the border strips, leaving a ¼"-wide seam allowance.

6. Repeat with the remaining corners.

## BASTING
■ ■ ■ ■ ■ ■ ■ ■ ■ ■ ■ ■ ■

To baste the quilt top, batting, and backing together with tailor tacks, use a long darning needle and a very long thread. Starting in the middle of the quilt and stitching toward yourself, take a stitch through all three layers, parallel to the edge of the quilt. Continue taking stitches parallel to the first stitch. The stitches you see on top will zigzag down the middle of the quilt. Baste the quilt in quarter sections.

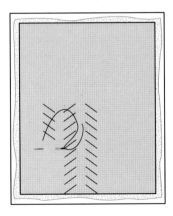

## BINDING

1. Once the project is completely quilted, trim the backing and batting to the size of the quilt top. Occasionally the quilting process will distort a quilt slightly, so make sure the corners are square, the quilt width is consistent from top to bottom, and the length is consistent from side to side.

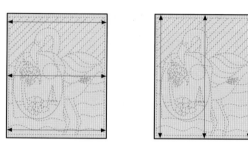

2. Cut 2" x 42" binding strips and sew them together end to end until the strip is long enough to go around the quilt, plus about 12". Trim the seam allowance and press open.

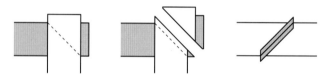

3. Press the entire strip in half lengthwise, wrong sides together.

4. Pin the binding strip to the front of the quilt, leaving a 12" length of the binding before starting to pin.

5. Begin stitching the binding to the quilt, using a ¼"-wide seam allowance. Stop ¼" before the first corner and remove the project from the sewing machine. Turn the quilt 90° and bring the binding strip straight up, and then down as shown. Begin stitching from the edge of the quilt.

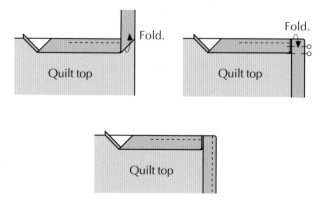

6. Continue stitching the binding to the quilt, until you are about 12" from where you began. Remove the quilt from the sewing machine.

7. Open the unsewn binding ends, lay them flat on the edge of the quilt, and bring the unsewn pieces together. Where the pieces meet, fold one end up at a 45° angle and the other end down at a 45° angle. Finger-press the folds.

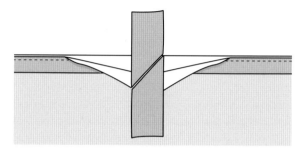

8. Bring the bottom binding up and align the folds, placing one end on top of the other. Pin the pieces together at the fold marks and stitch on the fold lines.

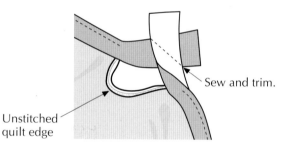

9. Before trimming the seam allowances, refold the binding in half lengthwise to make sure the binding fits the quilt exactly. Trim the seam allowance, refold the binding, and finish sewing it to the quilt.

10. Bring the binding over the raw edge to the back of the quilt and blindstitch in place. Be sure to stitch the small folds at the corners.

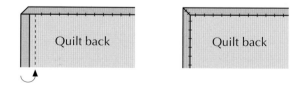

# FLAMINGO À LA ANDY

**Finished size: 66" x 78"**

Get out the rotary cutter and rev up the sewing machine.
This colorful Art Deco quilt would be a cheery addition to any room.
I was inspired by the work of Andy Warhol.

## MATERIALS: 42"-WIDE FABRIC

4½ yds. white for blocks and borders
    (2½ yds. for blocks only)
2 yds. pink
⅓ yd. yellow
1½ yds. black for blocks and binding
    (⅛ yd. for blocks only)
6 yds. backing
70" x 82" piece of thin batting

## CUTTING

Cut the white fabric into a 2-yard piece (set aside for borders) and a 2½-yard piece.

**From the lengthwise grain of the 2½-yard white piece, cut:**
2 strips, each 2⅛" x 60½"
2 strips, each 2⅜" x 51¾"
9 pieces, each 6½" x 9½"
18 pieces, each 4½" x 8½"
9 pieces, each 3½" x 4½"
9 squares, each 3½" x 3½"
9 pieces, each 2½" x 6½"
9 pieces, each 2½" x 4½"
45 squares, each 2½" x 2½"
9 pieces, each 1½" x 4½"
9 pieces, each 1½" x 2½"
36 squares, each 1½" x 1½"

**From the pink, cut:**
9 pieces, each 4½" x 12½"
9 pieces, each 2½" x 6½"
9 pieces, each 2½" x 14½"
9 pieces, each 2½" x 4½"
27 pieces, each 3½" x 6½"
9 squares, each 1½" x 1½"

**From the yellow, cut:**
9 pieces, each 2½" x 3½"
9 squares, each 2½" x 2½"
18 squares, each 1½" x 1½"

**From the black, cut:**
9 squares, each 1½" x 1½"

## MAKING THE FLAMINGO BLOCKS

1. Sew the 4½" x 8½" white rectangles to the 4½" x 12½" pink rectangles.

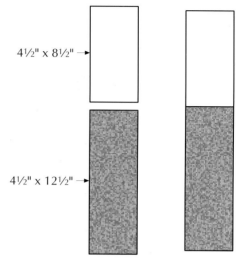

4½" x 8½" →

4½" x 12½" →

Make 9.

2. Using a sharp pencil, draw a line from corner to corner on the wrong side of each 2½" white square.
3. Place a square on one end of each 2½" x 14½" pink rectangle as shown. Sew on the marked line. Trim ¼" from the seam and press open.

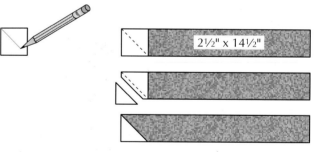

2½" x 14½"

Make 9.

4. Place a 2½" white square on each 2½" x 6½" pink piece; sew, trim, and press as shown.

Make 9.

5. Place a 1½" white square on the right corner of a pink 3½" x 6½" rectangle; sew, trim, and press. Make a mirror-image unit by stitching another 1½" white square to the left corner of a 3½" x 6½" pink rectangle.

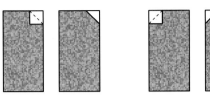

Make 9.　　　　Make 9.

6. Add a 4½" x 8½" white rectangle and a 2½" x 6½" white rectangle to the units made in steps 2–5.

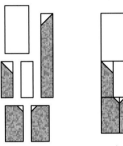

Make 9.

7. Draw a line from corner to corner on each 3½" white square. Place a white square on one end of a 3½" x 6½" pink rectangle; sew, trim, and press as shown.

Make 9.

8. Draw a line from corner to corner on the wrong side of a 1½" pink square. Place the pink square on a 2½" white square; sew, trim, and press.
9. Sew a 2½" white square to a 2½" x 4½" pink rectangle; trim and press. Sew the units together.

Make 9.　　　　Make 9.

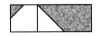

10. Draw a line from corner to corner on the wrong side of a 1½" white square. Place the white square on the lower left corner of a 2½" x 3½" yellow piece; sew, trim, and press.
11. Add a 3½" x 4½" white rectangle to the side as shown.

Make 9.

12. Draw a line from corner to corner on the wrong side of a 2½" yellow square. Place it on the end of a 2½" x 4½" white piece; sew, trim, and press.
13. On the yellow corner of the unit, place a 1½" white square; sew, trim, and press.

Make 9.

14. Place a yellow 1½" square on the corner of a white 2½" square; sew, trim and press. Sew this unit to the one made in steps 11 and 12.

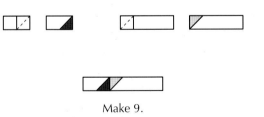

Make 9.

15. Sew a 1½" black square to the end of a 1½" x 2½" white piece.
16. Sew a 1½" yellow square to the end of a 1½" x 4½" white piece. Sew the units together as shown.

Make 9.

17. Assemble the units made in steps 7–15, adding a 6½" x 9½" white rectangle.

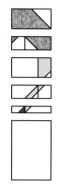

18. Sew the flamingo units together.

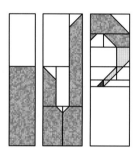

---

## ADDING THE BORDERS
■■■■■■■■■■■■■■■■■■■■■■■■■■

### Inner Borders

1. Sew the white 2⅛" x 60½" strips to the sides.
2. Sew the white 2⅜" x 51¾" strips to the top and bottom of the quilt top.

### Pieced Border

**From the remaining 2 yards of white, cut:**
9 strips, each 6¾" x 42"
1 strip, 1¾" x 42"
Reserve the remaining fabric for the fan blades.

**From the remaining black, cut:**
9 strips, each 1¾" x 42"
Reserve the remaining fabric for the fan blades and binding.

1. Sew together the 6¾"-wide white strips and the 1¾"-wide black strips to make 9 strip units. Press the seam allowances toward the black. Crosscut the units into a total of 190 pieced strips, each 1¾" wide.

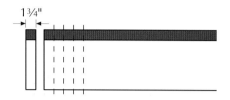

2. To make the top and bottom borders, sew together 41 pieced strips for each. Alternate the direction of the strips, starting and finishing with a black piece at the top. Press all seams in one direction.

3. Sew the top and bottom border strips to the quilt top, pinning at each seam. Be sure the borders are oriented as shown in the quilt diagram; black squares should appear at the corners. To prevent distortion as you add the borders, sew with the border strip on the bottom; the feed dogs will move the fabric along. Press the seam allowance toward the center.
4. For each side border, sew together 51 strips, starting and finishing with a black piece at the top. Press all seam allowances in one direction.
5. Using the template on page 16, cut 6 black fan blades and 4 white fan blades.
6. Sew the fan blades together as shown.

Make 2.

7. Sew 1 fan to the top of each side border. Be sure the right and left borders are oriented as shown in the quilt diagram; the black squares should meet the fans at the outer edges.

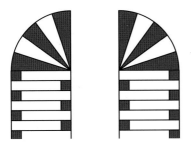

8. From the remaining 1¾"-wide white strip, cut 4 strips, each 1¾" x 8", and 6 squares, each 1¾" x 1¾". From the black scraps, cut 6 squares, each 1¾" x 1¾".

9. Sew 3 black and 3 white 1¾" squares together to make a checkerboard strip. Make 2 strips.

Make 2.

10. Use the remaining pieced border strips, the 8"-long white strips, and the checkerboard strips to make 2 blocks as shown.

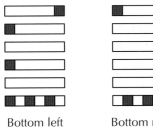

Bottom left          Bottom right
corner                 corner

11. Sew the blocks to the bottoms of the side borders, and then sew the borders to the quilt top. Press the seam allowances toward the quilt.

---

## FINISHING
■■■■■■■■■■■■■

1. Layer the quilt top with batting and backing.
2. Baste, and then quilt as desired.
3. Bind the edges, using bias-cut strips to ensure smooth curves.
4. Label your quilt.

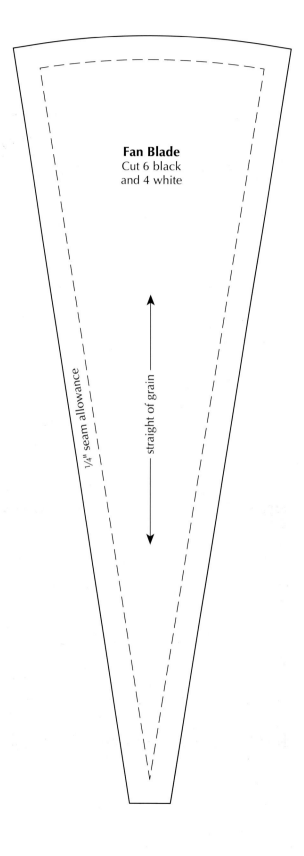

**Fan Blade**
Cut 6 black
and 4 white

¼" seam allowance

straight of grain

# GALLERY

## DEFINITELY DECO

By Marilyn Dorwart, 1996, Delray Beach, Florida, 40" x 45". Instructions begin on page 38.

## THE MARKETPLACE

By Marilyn Dorwart, 1996, Delray Beach,
Florida, 63" x 40". Instructions
begin on page 63.

## A FLORIDA DREAM

By Marilyn Dorwart, 1996, Delray Beach,
Florida, 31" x 37". Instructions
begin on page 51.

# FLAMINGO À LA ANDY

By Marilyn Dorwart, 1996, Delray Beach, Florida, 66" x 78". Instructions begin on page 11.

## A FIELD OF LILIES

By Marilyn Dorwart, 1996, Delray Beach,
Florida, 61" x 88". Instructions
begin on page 25.

## TIGER LILY

By Marilyn Dorwart,
1996, Delray Beach, Florida.
You can replace the flower
in the quilt shown at left
with this Tiger Lily
if you prefer.
Pattern on page 33.

## TULIPS IN THE WIND

By Marilyn Dorwart, 1996, Delray Beach,
Florida, 58" x 89". Instructions
begin on page 29.

IN MY LADY'S GARDEN

By Marilyn Dorwart, 1993, Delray Beach, Florida, 64" x 45". Instructions begin on page 54.

## CHILI PEPPER WREATH

By Marilyn Dorwart, 1996, Delray Beach, Florida, 50" x 50". Instructions begin on page 34.

## LUNCH TIME

By Marilyn Dorwart, 1996, Delray Beach, Florida, 35" x 47". Instructions begin on page 47.

COASTAL COLLAGE

By Marilyn Dorwart, 1996, Delray Beach, Florida, 30" x 38". Instructions begin on page 45.

# A FIELD OF LILIES

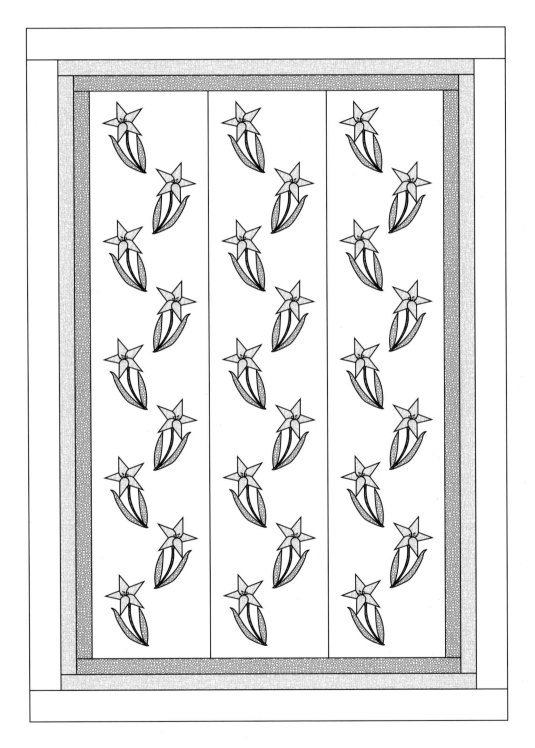

A combination of yellow, green,
and white would look fresh.

## Yardage Requirements: 42"-wide fabric

| | Crib | Twin | Queen | King |
|---|---|---|---|---|
| | 42" x 57" | 61" x 88" | 84" x 104" | 120" x 120" |
| Flowers | ⅛ each of 5 fabrics | ¼ each of 5 fabrics | ½ each of 5 fabrics | ¾ each of 5 fabrics |
| Stems | ¼ | ¼ | ⅓ | ¾ |
| Leaves | ¼ | ½ | ¾ | 1 |
| Background and outer border | 2 | 4½ | 5 | 8 |
| Inner border | ¼ | ¾ | 1¼ | 1½ |
| Middle border | ½ | 1 | 1½ | 2 |
| Backing | 2 | 5 | 6 | 10½ |
| Binding | ½ | ½ | ¾ | 1¼ |
| Batting | 46" x 61" | 65" x 92" | 88" x 108" | 124" x 124" |

Additional Materials: Black embroidery floss

## Cutting

**Read "Appliquéing the Quilt Top" below before cutting out the appliqué pieces.**

Cut the background panels on the lengthwise grain.

| Piece | Number to Cut | | | |
|---|---|---|---|---|
| | Crib | Twin | Queen | King |
| Templates 1–6 | 15 | 27 | 40 | 72 |
| Templates 7 & 8 | 15 & 15r | 27 & 27r | 40 & 40r | 72 & 72r |
| Background panels | 2, each 16½" x 46½" | 3, each 16½" x 73½" | 4, each 16½" x 81½" | 6, each 16½" x 91½" |
| Flowers per panel | 5 | 9 | 10 | 12 |

## APPLIQUÉING THE QUILT TOP

*Refer to "Preassembled Appliqué" on pages 6–7.*

Use the pattern on page 28 to make templates for pieces 1–8. With minor adjustments to your yardage and cutting, you can use the Tiger Lily pattern on page 33 if you prefer.

1. Using Preassembled-Appliqué Technique 2, appliqué pieces 1–5 to each other in numerical order. Keep the fabrics in the same order for each flower.

2. Embroider the filaments with a stem stitch and make a French knot at the top of each.

3. Prepare pieces 6–8 for appliqué.

4. Referring to the cutting chart for the correct number, evenly space the flowers on the first panel and pin them in place. Alternate the orientation of the stems and leaves. Appliqué the leaves, then the stems and petal units. To check the placement of the flowers on the second and third panels, lay each panel on top of the first panel, and then place the flowers, stems, and leaves over the flowers on the first panel. (Tape the panels to a window or use a light box for better visibility.)

5. Trim the panels to the required size.
   Crib: 15½" x 45½"
   Twin: 15½" x 72½"
   Queen: 15½" x 80½"
   King: 15½" x 90½"

6. Sew the panels together lengthwise.

## Cutting for Borders

Sew strips together as necessary to make borders of the required length.

| No. to Cut | Dimensions | | | |
|---|---|---|---|---|
| | **Crib** | **Twin** | **Queen** | **King** |
| **Inner Border** | | | | |
| 2 strips | 1½" x 45½" | 2½" x 72½" | 3½" x 80½" | 4½" x 90½" |
| 2 strips | 1½" x 32½" | 2½" x 49½" | 3½" x 66½" | 4½" x 98½" |
| **Middle Border** | | | | |
| 2 strips | 2½" x 47½" | 2½" x 76½" | 4½" x 86½" | 5½" x 98½" |
| 2 strips | 2½" x 36½" | 2½" x 53½" | 4½" x 74½" | 5½" x 108½" |
| **Outer Border** | | | | |
| 2 strips | 3½" x 42½" | 4½" x 80½" | 5½" x 94½" | 6½" x 108½" |
| 2 strips | 3½" x 42½" | 4½" x 61½" | 5½" x 84½" | 6½" x 120½" |

## ADDING THE BORDERS

1. For the inner border, sew the 2 longest strips to the sides of the quilt top, and then sew the remaining strips to the top and bottom.
2. For the outer border, sew the 2 longest strips to the sides of the quilt top, and then sew the remaining strips to the top and bottom.

## FINISHING

1. Layer the quilt top with batting and backing.
2. Baste, and then quilt as desired.
3. Label your quilt.

### Quilting Suggestion

*To fill the background, quilt diagonal lines in both directions. Quilt ¼" from each side of the border seams, and then quilt scallops or cables in the borders.*

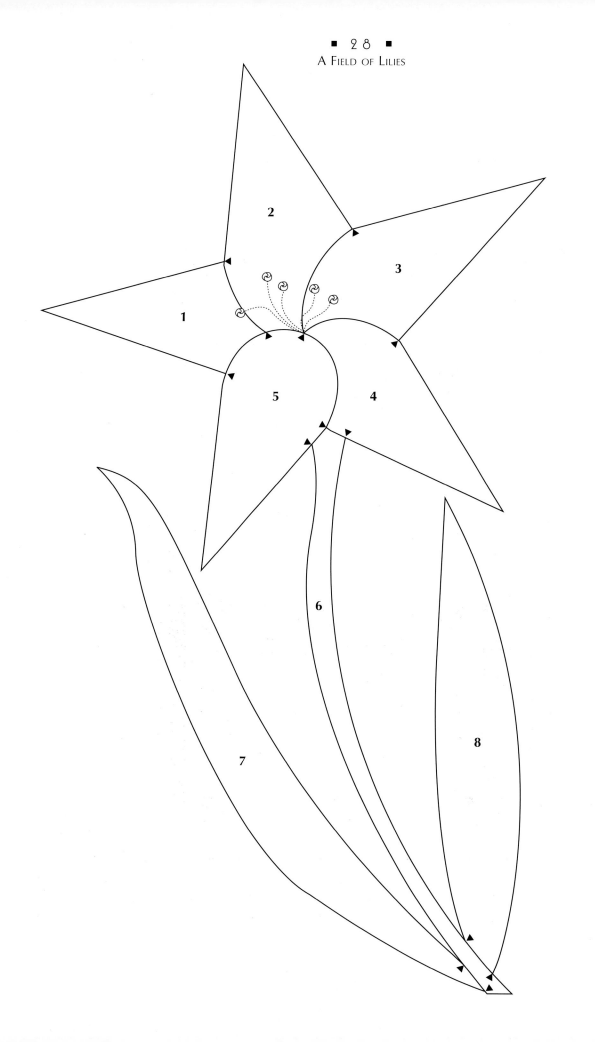

# TULIPS IN THE WIND

Growing up in Minnesota, tulips greeted me
every spring. There are so many colors
in the tulip family that this quilt
could sing with a variety of lively hues.

## Yardage Requirements: 42"-wide fabric

| | Crib | Twin | Queen | King |
|---|---|---|---|---|
| | 42" x 59" | 61" x 84" | 84" x 107" | 114" x 124" |
| Center flower petal | ⅛ | ¼ | ⅓ | ½ |
| Side flower petals | ¼ | ⅓ | ½ | ⅔ |
| Flower petal tips | ⅛ | ¼ | ⅓ | ½ |
| Dark green for stems | ⅓ | ½ | ¾ | 1 |
| 2 medium greens for leaves | ⅓ total | ¾ total | 1 total | 1½ total |
| Background & border | 2 | 4½ | 5 | 8 |
| Green for first border | ½ | ⅔ | 1 | 1¼ |
| Red for second border | ½ | 1 | 1½ | 2 |
| Backing | 1⅔ | 5 | 6 | 10½ |
| Batting | 46" x 63" | 65" x 88" | 88" x 111" | 118" x 128" |

## Cutting

Read "Appliquéing the Quilt Top" below before cutting out the appliqué pieces.

| Piece | Number to Cut | | | |
|---|---|---|---|---|
| | Crib | Twin | Queen | King |
| Templates 1–4, 7 | 14 | 30 | 48 | 78 |
| Templates 5, 6, 8 | 14, 14r | 33, 33r | 48, 48r | 78, 78r |
| Background panels | 2, each 16½" x 48½" | 3, each 16½" x 69½" | 4, each 16½" x 84½" | 6, each 16½" x 95½" |
| Flowers per panel | 7 | 10 | 12 | 13 |

## APPLIQUÉING THE QUILT TOP

*Refer to "Preassembled Appliqué" on pages 6–7.*
Use the tulip pattern on page 32 to make templates for pieces 1–8.

1. Using Preassembled-Appliqué Technique 2, appliqué pieces 1–4 to each other in numerical order. Cutting template 1 as shown makes it easier to appliqué petal 2 and assures that the petal units will be uniform in shape.

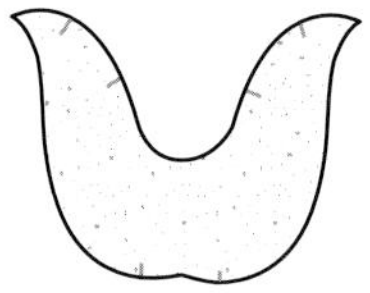

Template 1

2. Using Preassembled-Appliqué Technique 1, construct leaf units from templates 5 and 6. Prepare the template 8 leaves for appliqué.

3. Referring to the cutting chart for the correct number, evenly space the flowers on 1 panel and pin in place. Alternate the orientation of the leaves and stems. Appliqué the leaves to the background, then the stems and the petal units. To check the placement of the flowers on the second and third panels, lay each on top of the first panel and place the flowers, stems, and leaves over the flowers on the first panel. (Tape the panels to a window or use a light box for better visibility.)

4. Trim the panels to the required size.
   Crib: 15½" x 47½"
   Twin: 15½" x 68½"
   Queen: 15½" x 83½"
   King: 15½" x 94½"

5. Sew the panels together lengthwise.

## Cutting for Borders

Sew strips together as necessary to make borders of the required length.

| | Crib | Twin | Queen | King |
|---|---|---|---|---|
| **First Border** | | | | |
| 2 strips | 2½" x 47½" | 2½" x 68½" | 4½" x 83½" | 5½" x 94½" |
| 2 strips | 2½" x 34½" | 2½" x 49½" | 4½" x 68½" | 5½" x 100½" |
| **Second Border** | | | | |
| 2 strips | 1½" x 51½" | 2" x 72½" | 3½" x 91½" | 4½" x 104½" |
| 2 strips | 1½" x 36½" | 2" x 51½" | 3½" x 74½" | 4½" x 108½" |
| **Third Border** | | | | |
| 2 strips | 3½" x 53½" | 5" x 75½" | 5½" x 97½" | 6½" x 108½" |
| 2 strips | 3½" x 42½" | 5" x 60½" | 5½" x 84½" | 6½" x 120½" |

## ADDING THE BORDERS

1. For the first border, sew the 2 longest strips to the sides of the quilt top, and then sew the remaining strips to the top and bottom.
2. For the second border, sew the 2 longest strips to the sides of the quilt top, and then sew the remaining strips to the top and bottom.
3. For the third border, sew the 2 longest strips to the sides of the quilt top, and then sew the remaining strips to the top and bottom.

## FINISHING

1. Layer the quilt top with batting and backing.
2. Baste, and then quilt as desired.
3. Label your quilt.

### Quilting Suggestion

*Outline-quilt all the appliqué motifs. To fill the background, quilt diagonal lines in both directions, 2" apart. Quilt ¼" from each side of the border seams, and then quilt scallops or cables in the borders.*

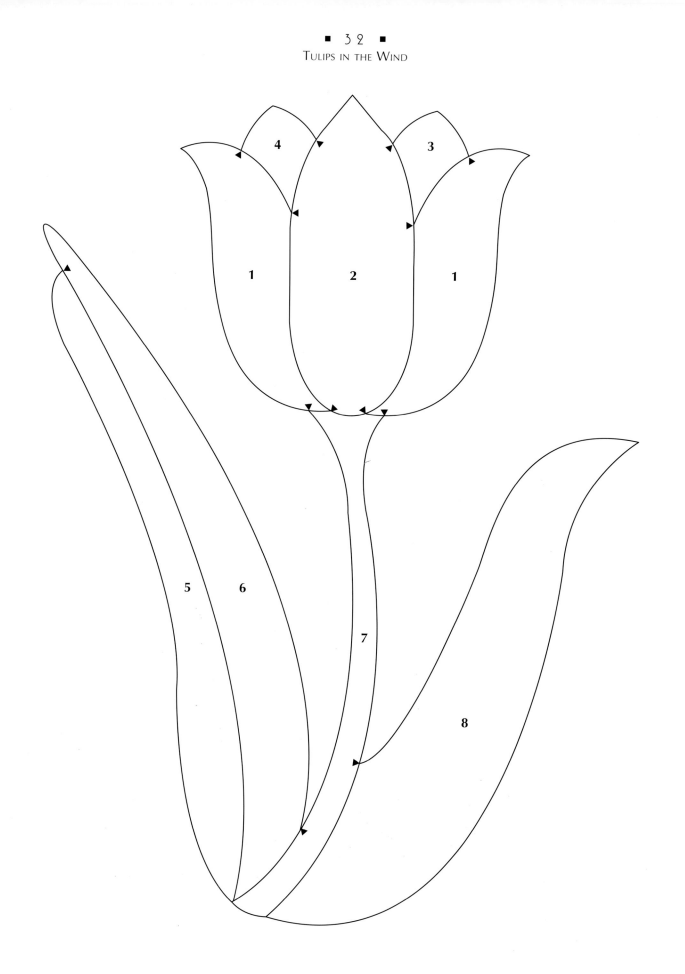

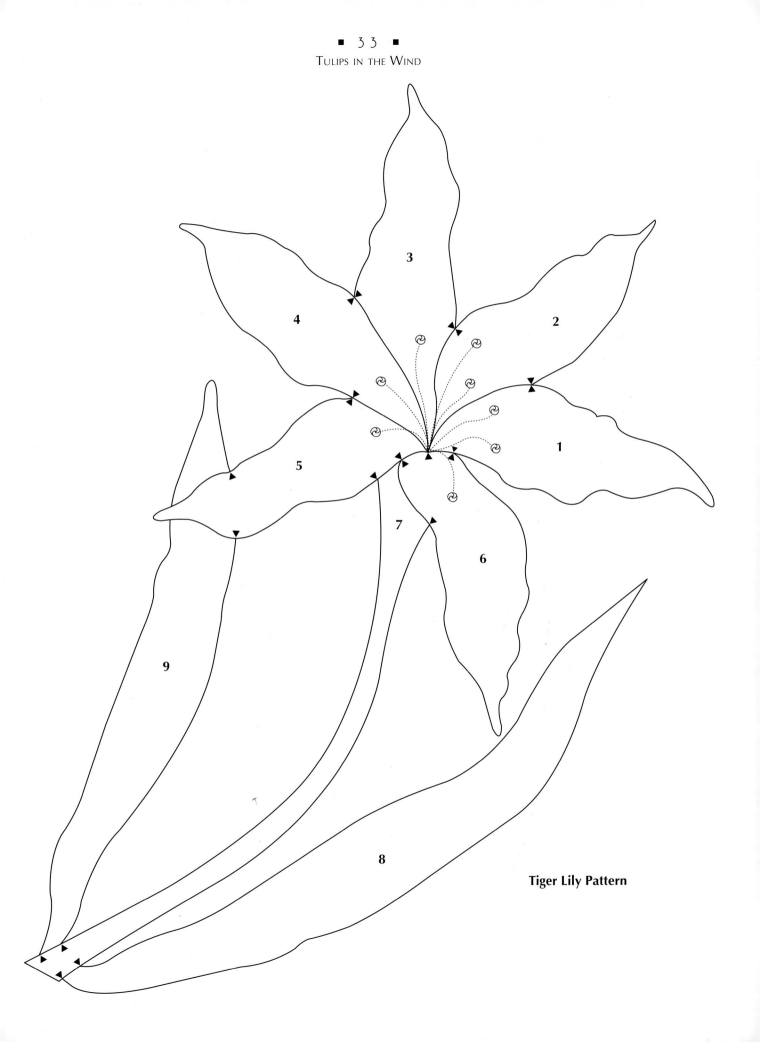

**Tiger Lily Pattern**

# CHILI PEPPER WREATH

**Finished size: 50" x 50"**

This wall hanging was inspired by a favorite restaurant of mine called Splendid Blendeds, where peppers of all varieties figure prominently on the menu. The Preassembled-Appliqué Techniques and your creativity are required for this project.

## MATERIALS: 42"-WIDE FABRIC

1¼ yds. for background
¼ yd. *each* of 6 reds for peppers
¼ yd. *each* of 6 greens for stems and leaves
⅛ yd. white for flowers
¼ yd. *each* of 5 yellows for peppers and
   flower centers
¼ yd. gold for prairie points
¼ yd. dark green for inner border
1½ yds. medium green for outer border
   and binding
3 yds. for backing
54" x 54" piece of thin batting

## CUTTING

*Read "Appliquéing the Quilt Top," which follows,
before cutting out the appliqué pieces.*

### From the background fabric, cut:
1 square, 42" x 42"

### From the reds, cut:
48 to 60 peppers, using any combination
of pepper templates 1–5

### From the greens, cut:
28 leaves, using any combination of the
   flower and pepper leaf templates
1 pepper-top template for each red and
   yellow pepper template

### From the white, cut:
5 full flowers
5 half flowers

### From the yellows, cut:
36 peppers, using any combination
   of pepper templates 1–5
5 full-flower centers
5 half-flower centers

### From the gold, cut:
50 squares, each 2" x 2"

### From the dark green, cut:
2 strips, each 1½" x 40½"
2 strips, each 1½" x 42½"*

### From the lengthwise grain of the medium green, cut:
2 strips, each 4½" x 43½"*
2 strips, each 4½" x 49½"*

*Piece strips as necessary to get the required length.

## APPLIQUÉING THE QUILT TOP

*Refer to "Preassembled Appliqué" on pages 6–7.*

1. Using Preassembled-Appliqué Technique 1, make
   the pepper units. Using any combination of
   pepper templates 1–5, trace 8 to 10 peppers onto
   each of the red fabrics, leaving room for pepper
   tops and seam allowances. Prepare a green top
   for each pepper. Appliqué the tops onto the red
   peppers traced on the fabric, and then cut out the
   red portion of the pepper unit. Use the same
   method to prepare 36 yellow peppers.

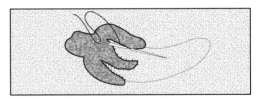

2. Using Preassembled-Appliqué Technique 1, make
   the full-flower and half-flower units. Trace 5 full
   flowers and 5 half flowers onto the white fabric.
   Appliqué the appropriate yellow center onto each
   traced petal piece, and then cut out the flower,
   adding a ⅛"-wide seam allowance.

3. Fold the square of background fabric in half and in half again; press lightly to mark the center. Measure about 6" out from the center and draw a circle, using a quilter's disappearing-ink marker or a chalk marker. Draw another circle, about 15" from the center. You will arrange the peppers, flowers, and leaves within these lines, but the appliqués may not cover them completely.

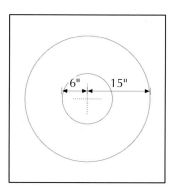

4. Using the photograph on page 22 as a guide, place the peppers, flowers, half flowers, and leaves in the wreath area. Overlap the appliqués, remembering that they will shrink when you turn under the seam allowances. Find a wall where you can temporarily attach the wall hanging to see if it is symmetrical, full enough, and generally pleasing to your eye. You may find that you want more peppers of one color or another, or you may want more flowers and leaves. Play with the arrangement until you are satisfied, and then pin the appliqués in place. Taking a double bite with the pin ensures that the pieces are held in place securely.

5. Appliqué the peppers, flowers, and leaves to the background, beginning with the pieces on the bottom layer and working upward. You may find it helpful to keep several needles going at the same time.

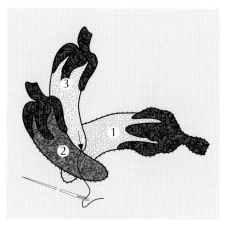

1. Appliqué completely.
2. Appliqué to this point, then put needle aside.

3. Begin appliquéing Pepper 3.
4. When you reach this point, put the needle aside and begin appliquéing Pepper 4.

## Tip

*When appliquéing overlapping pieces like the peppers, it is impossible to complete one without running into another. Appliqué the portion that does not lie under another piece. When you run into another piece, start a new needle and thread, leaving the first needle pinned to the fabric, out of your way. Appliqué the overlapping piece; then return to finish the first. Where many pieces overlap, you may need to start several threads before returning to the first piece.*

6. Trim the background to 38" x 40½".
7. Fold each gold square in half diagonally to create a triangle and press firmly. Fold in half again diagonally, and then press to make prairie points. Beginning in the upper left corner of the background square, place 11 prairie points down the side edge and 14 across the top, aligning raw edges. Space the points evenly. Place 11 prairie points along the lower right edge and 14 across the bottom. Sew the prairie points to the background, using a ¼"-wide seam allowance.

8. Sew the 1½" x 40½" dark green strips to the sides of the quilt top, sandwiching the prairie points between the background and the strip. Add the 1½" x 42½" strips to the top and bottom. Press the seam allowances toward the center of the quilt, the prairie points will lie flat against the inner border, pointing outward.
9. Sew the 4½" x 42½" medium green strips to the sides of the quilt top; sew the 4½" x 50½" strips to the top and bottom.

---

## FINISHING

1. Layer the quilt top with batting and backing.
2. Baste, and then quilt as desired.
3. Label your quilt.

## Quilting Suggestion

*Outline-quilt the wreath appliqués. Quilt a grid of diagonal lines, each 1" apart, in the background. Quilt Vs in the outer border to echo the prairie points.*

# DEFINITELY DECO

**Finished size: 46" x 50"**

Some well-known symbols of the tropical south, the Art Deco
borders, and lots of bright colors make an exciting wall hanging.

## MATERIALS: 42"-WIDE FABRIC

½ yd. *each* of 5 different blues for sky
   backgrounds
¼ yd. dark blue
¼ yd. light green for background
⅛ yd. brown for tree trunk
¼ yd. *each* of 3 yellows for sun and borders
¼ yd. *each* of 2 greens for palm fronds and
   sea grapes
¼ yd. *each* of 2 hot pinks for flower
¼ yd. murky green for alligator
⅜ yd. blue-green
⅜ yd. medium pink
⅜ yd. light pink
¼ yd. turquoise
¼ yd. light yellow
¼ yd. bright green
⅜ yd. orange
⅜ yd. light lavender
⅜ yd. light blue
½ yd. white for sailboat and side border
⅛ yd. light gray for heron
⅛ yd. white for sandpiper
¼ yd. black-and-white check for inner border
Scraps of greens, yellows, purple, orange,
   off-white, blacks, browns, white, red,
   organdy, grays, tan, pinks, mauve, aqua,
   gold, and peach
44" x 49" piece of thin batting
Dark red silk ribbon for sea grapes
Embroidery floss that gradates from dark red to
   gold for sea grape, gold for flower, black for
   sailboat and sandpiper, gray or green for grass

## CUTTING

*Number the blue fabrics for the
sky backgrounds 1–5.*

**From sky background 1, cut:**
2 squares, each 5½" x 5½",
for Orange block and border
1 piece, 9½" x 13½", for Lighthouse block
1 square, 13½" x 13½", for Flower block

**From sky background 2, cut:**
1 square, 5½" x 5½", for border
1 piece, 5½" x 13½", for Seashell block
1 square, 9½" x 9½", for Sun block
1 piece, 13½" x 25½", for Sailboat block

**From sky background 3, cut:**
1 square, 5½" x 5½", for border
1 piece, 5½" x 13½", for Sea Grape block
1 piece, 13½" x 21½", for Palm Tree block

**From sky background 4, cut:**
1 square, 5½" x 5½", for border
2 pieces, each 9½" x 13½",
for Sandpiper and Heron blocks

**From sky background 5, cut:**
1 piece, 5½" x 17½", for Bird of Paradise block
1 piece, 5½" x 37½", for Wave block

**From the dark blue, cut:**
1 strip, 5½" x 37½", for wave

**From the light green, cut:**
1 strip, 5½" x 25½", for Alligator block

**From the brown, cut:**
1 strip, ½" x 22", for sailboat mast

## APPLIQUÉING THE BLOCKS

*Use the templates on the pullout and on pages 43–44.
Refer to "Preassembled Appliqué" on pages 6–7.*

### Sun Block

Using appropriate fabrics, prepare and appliqué
pieces 1–3 as follows.
1. Using Preassembled-Appliqué Technique 2,
   appliqué the sun center (piece 1) to the points
   (piece 2). Appliqué the points to the outer disk
   (piece 3).
2. Appliqué the completed sun to the 9½" square of
   sky background 2. Trim the sky background to
   8½" x 8½".
3. Carefully trim away the background fabric behind
   the sun.

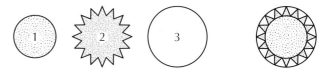

## Lighthouse Block

Use Preassembled-Appliqué Technique 2 to make the lighthouse. Using appropriate fabrics, prepare and appliqué pieces 1–11 as follows.

1. Appliqué the black stripes (pieces 2, 3, and 4) to the white base (piece 1) of the lighthouse.
2. Appliqué pieces 5–9 to each other to form the top of the lighthouse.
3. Appliqué the top of the lighthouse to the bottom.
4. Pin the lighthouse to the 9½" x 13½" piece of sky background 1, and appliqué in place.
5. Appliqué piece 10, then piece 11, to cover the bottom of the lighthouse.
6. Embroider details with a stem stitch and a straight stitch. Trim the background to 8½" x 12½".

## Palm Tree Block

Using appropriate fabrics, prepare and appliqué pieces 1–8. Appliqué the tree trunk and palm fronds to the 13½" x 21½" piece of sky background 3 in numerical order. Trim the block background to 12½" x 20½".

## Bird of Paradise Block

Using appropriate fabrics, prepare and appliqué pieces 1–9. Appliqué the pieces to the 5½" x 17½" piece of sky background 5 in numerical order. Trim the block background to 4½" x 16½".

## Sailboat Block

Using appropriate fabrics, prepare and appliqué pieces 1–3 as follows.

1. Using Preassembled-Appliqué Technique 1, appliqué the trim to the boat.
2. Pin the boat and sails to the 13½" x 25½" piece of sky background 2. Position the mast between the sails and appliqué the pieces to the background.
3. Appliqué the flag to the top of the mast
4. Embroider rigging lines with a stem stitch.
5. Trim the block background to 12½" x 24½".

## Heron Block

Using appropriate fabrics, prepare the pieces on page 43 and appliqué as follows.

1. Using Preassembled-Appliqué Technique 1, appliqué the beak, wing, and legs to the body.
2. Appliqué the completed bird onto a 9½" x 13½" piece of background 4. Embroider the eye with a French knot, the topknot with a stem stitch, the beak detail with a satin stitch, and the grass with a stem stitch. Trim the block background to 8½" x 12½".

## Seashells and Starfish Block

Using appropriate fabrics, prepare the shell and starfish pieces and appliqué as follows.

1. Using Preassembled-Appliqué Technique 1, make 2 of shell 1. Cut out the shell (piece 1), adding a ¼"-wide seam allowance, and reverse-appliqué it to the center (piece 2). Cut out the entire shell, adding a ⅛"-wide seam allowance.
2. Using Preassembled-Appliqué Technique 2, make shell 2. Cut out piece 1, adding a ½"-wide seam allowance. Cut out each successive piece, adding a ½"-wide seam allowance and appliquéing it to the piece before, until you reach piece 9. Add a ⅛"-wide seam allowance to piece 9 and appliqué it to piece 8.
3. Appliqué the completed shells and the starfish to the 5½" x 13½" piece of sky background 2. Trim the block background to 4½" x 12½".

## Alligator Block

Using appropriate fabrics, prepare and appliqué pieces 1–7 as follows.

1. Using Preassembled-Appliqué Technique 2, appliqué the alligator pieces to the body in numerical order. Appliqué the completed alligator to the 5½" x 25½" light green background.
2. For more definition, outline the teeth with green or gold embroidery floss in a stem stitch.
3. Trim the block background to 4½" x 24½".

## Orange Block

Using appropriate fabrics, prepare and appliqué pieces 1–4. Appliqué the stem, leaves, and orange to the 5½" square of sky background 1 in numerical order. Trim the block background to 4½" x 4½".

## Sandpiper Block

Use Preassembled-Appliqué Technique 1 to make the Sandpiper block. Using appropriate fabrics, prepare and appliqué pieces 1–3 as follows.

1. Trace piece 1 onto the white fabric. Cut out pieces 2 and 3 and appliqué them to piece 1. Cut out the completed body.
2. Position 1 sandpiper on each half of the 9½" x 13½" sky background 4, and then appliqué the sandpipers in place.
3. Trace the legs, beaks, and grass onto the background. Use black embroidery floss and a satin stitch for the legs and beak; make French knots for the eyes. Use gray or green embroidery floss and a stem stitch for the grass. Trim to 8½" x 12½".

## Sea Grapes Block

Using appropriate fabrics, prepare and appliqué pieces 1–11 as follows.

1. Appliqué the stem and leaves to the 5½" x 13½" piece of sky background 3.
2. Using the stem stitch, embroider the remaining stems and the leaf veins. For the berries, make French knots with the silk ribbon.
3. Trim the block background to 4½" x 12½".

## Large Flower Block

Using appropriate fabrics, prepare and appliqué pieces 1–12 as follows.

1. Using Preassembled-Appliqué Technique 2, appliqué pieces 1–5 of the large flower to each other in numerical order.
2. Appliqué stem piece 9 to the flower, then piece 10.
3. Appliqué the bud pieces to each other in numerical order, and then appliqué the stem to the bud.
4. Appliqué the completed unit to the 13½" square of sky background 1, and then add the large leaf.
5. Embroider the flower centers, using a stem stitch and French knots. Trim the block background to 12½" x 12½".

## CUTTING BORDER STRIPS

**From the fabric for the inner border, cut:**
2 strips, each 1½" x 40½"
2 strips, each 1½" x 38½"

**From the blue-green, pink,
light blue, and light pink, cut:**
2 strips from *each* fabric, each 4½" x 42",
for a total of 8 strips.* Sew the matching strips together; then trim each pieced strip to 4½" x 42½", for a total of 4 strips.
*If your fabric is wider than 42½",
cut only 1 strip from each color.*

**From the light yellow, orange,
bright green, and light lavender, cut:**
1 strip from *each* fabric, each 4½" x 38½",
for a total of 4 strips

## ASSEMBLING THE QUILT

1. Sew the blocks together as shown.

2. Make a plastic template of the wave on the pullout. Place the template at the left end of the dark blue strip with the bottom edge on the edge of the fabric, and draw lightly around it. Move the template to the right, and repeat until there are 8 waves across the length of the fabric.

3. Cut around the top of the wave, adding a ¼"-wide seam allowance, and pin the wave strip to the 4½" x 36½" sky background 5 strip, aligning the lower edges. Appliqué the upper edge in place. Sew this strip to the lower edge of the quilt top.

4. Sew the 1½" x 40½" inner-border strips to the sides of the quilt top, and then sew the 1½" x 38½" strips to the top and bottom.

5. Accordion-fold the pink and blue-green 4½" x 42½" strips. Place the border zigzag template on the top fold, mark, and cut through all the layers at once.

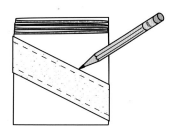

6. Open the zigzag strips, and pin each to a 4½" x 42½" background strip (light blue for the pink, light pink for the blue-green), and appliqué.

7. Prepare the border triangle and border half-circle templates on the pullout, and cut out 6 triangles and 8 half-circles from scraps of assorted colors. Appliqué them in place as shown in the quilt diagram. Align the outer edges with the edges of the strips and leave them unsewn. Sew the strips to the sides of the quilt top.

8. Make a plastic template of the border curve. Place the template on the left end of the orange 4½" x 38½" strip. Trace the inner and outer edges of the curve, ending exactly at the corners. Flip the template over and position it right next to the

ends of the lines you just drew. Trace the edges as before. Continue flipping the template and tracing along the edges to create the curve motif. Repeat with the 4½" x 38½" bright green strip.

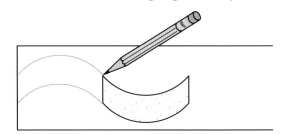

9. Cut out the curved strips, adding ⅛"-wide seam allowances. Pin them to the background strips (light yellow for the orange and light lavender for the bright green), and appliqué.

10. Using the border circle on the pullout, prepare circles for appliqué from scraps of assorted colors. Appliqué circles on both sides of the curved strips as shown in the quilt diagram.

11. Using the medium corner circle on the pullout and the large corner circle on page 44, prepare corner circles from scraps of assorted colors. Appliqué a small circle to each large circle, and then appliqué a circle unit to each remaining 5½" blue square. Trim the squares to 4½" x 4½".

12. Sew the 4½" x 42½" strips to the sides of the quilt top.

13. Sew a corner square to each end of the 4½" x 38½" border strips. Sew the pieced strips to the top and bottom of the quilt top.

## FINISHING

1. Layer the quilt top with batting and backing.
2. Baste, and then quilt as desired.
3. Label your quilt.

### Quilting Suggestion

*Outline-quilt each of the appliqué motifs.*

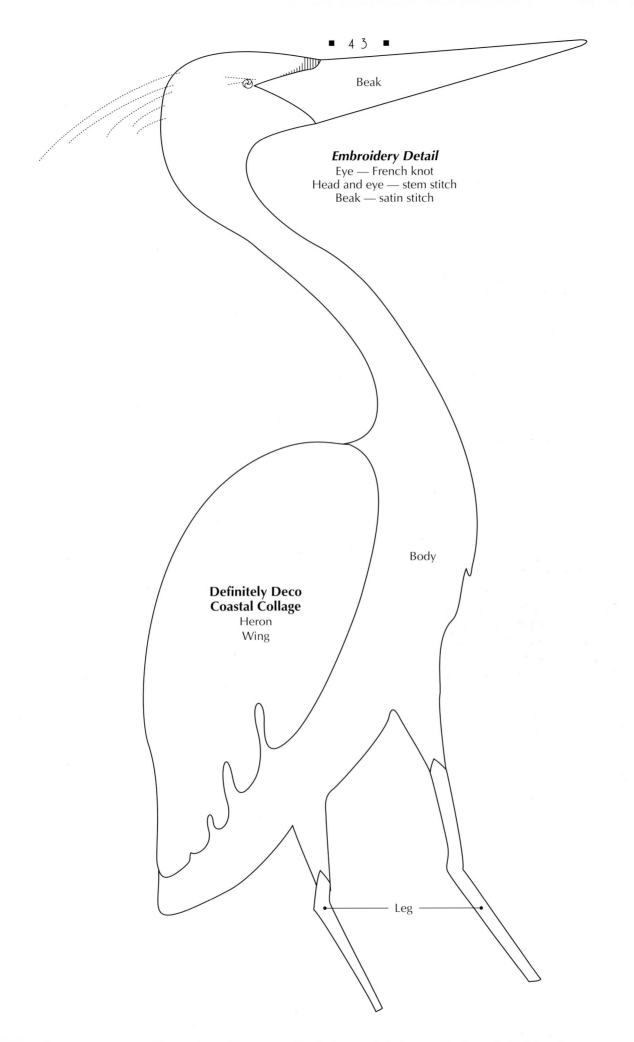

Beak

***Embroidery Detail***
Eye — French knot
Head and eye — stem stitch
Beak — satin stitch

Body

**Definitely Deco
Coastal Collage**
Heron
Wing

Leg

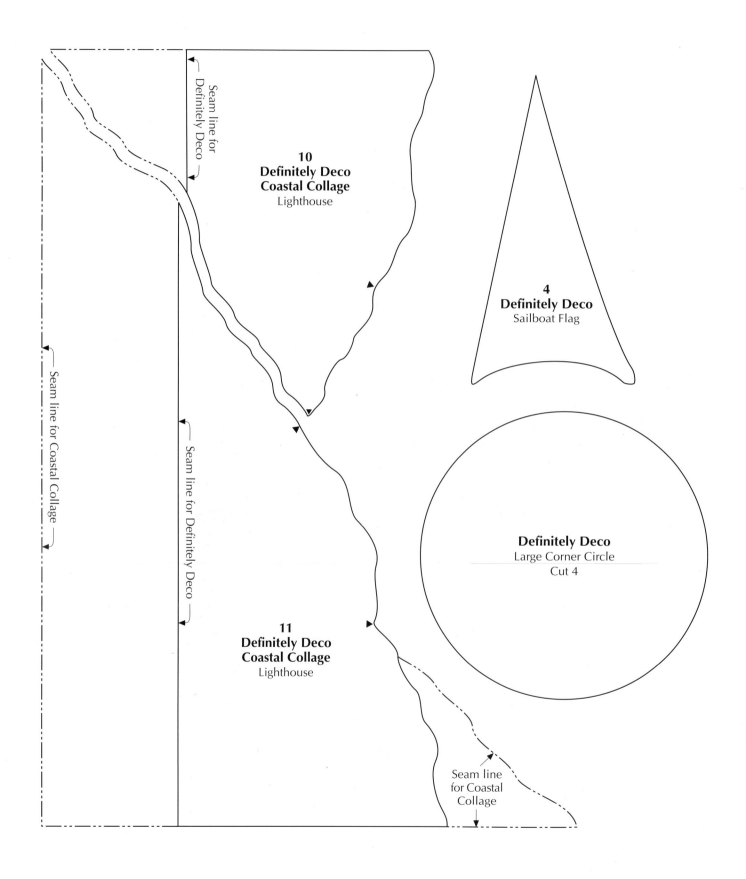

Seam line for
Definitely Deco

**10
Definitely Deco
Coastal Collage**
Lighthouse

**4
Definitely Deco**
Sailboat Flag

Seam line for Coastal Collage

Seam line for Definitely Deco

**Definitely Deco**
Large Corner Circle
Cut 4

**11
Definitely Deco
Coastal Collage**
Lighthouse

Seam line
for Coastal
Collage

# COASTAL COLLAGE

**Finished size: 30" x 38"**

The recipe for this wall hanging is four blocks from
"Definitely Deco," a sprinkle of Northern color,
and a dash of stormy weather.

## MATERIALS: 42"-WIDE FABRIC

½ yd. black for inner borders
½ yd. for outer border
⅓ yd. *each* of 2 blue fabrics for Lighthouse and Heron block backgrounds
¼ yd. *each* of 2 blue fabrics for Seashells and Starfish and the Sandpiper block backgrounds
¼ yd. gray for rocks
⅛ yd. white for sandpipers and heron (You may want to use 2 different whites.)
1 yd. for backing
Scraps of 3 tans for shells, gold for heron beak and legs, black, white, gray and red for lighthouse, tan and brown for sandpipers
34" x 42" piece of thin batting
Black and gold embroidery floss

## CUTTING

**From the black, cut:**
2 strips, each 2½" x 10½", for sashing
1 strip, 2½" x 20½", for sashing
1 strip, 4½" x 8½", for sashing
2 strips, each 1½" x 26½", for inner border
2 strips, each 2½" x 22½", for inner border

**From the fabric for the outer border, cut:**
4 strips, each 4½" x 30½"

**From the blue for the Lighthouse and Heron blocks, cut:**
1 piece, 9½" x 17½", for Lighthouse block
1 piece, 11½" x 13½", for Heron block

**From the blue for the Seashells and Starfish and the Sandpiper block backgrounds, cut:**
1 piece, 7½" x 21½", for Sandpiper block
1 piece, 5½" x 11½", for Seashells and Starfish block

## APPLIQUÉING THE BLOCKS

To make the Lighthouse, Heron, Sandpiper, and Seashells and Starfish blocks, refer to "Appliquéing the Blocks" (Definitely Deco) on pages 39–41, with the following changes.

Lighthouse block: Use the larger rock template for the foreground. Trim to 8½" x 16½".
Sandpiper block: Make 3 birds instead of 2. Trim to 6½" x 20½".
Seashells and Starfish block: Make 2 shells of your choice and 1 starfish. Trim to 4½" x 10½".

## ASSEMBLING THE QUILT TOP

1. Assemble the quilt top as shown.

2. Sew the 1½" x 26½" black strips to the sides of the quilt top, and then sew the 2½" x 22½" black strips to the top and bottom.
3. Sew the 4½" x 30½" outer-border strips to the sides of the quilt top, and then sew the 4½" x 30½" strips to the top and bottom.
4. Using a stem stitch and running stitch, embroider grass around the heron and the sandpipers.

## FINISHING

1. Layer the quilt top with batting and backing
2. Baste, and then quilt as desired.
3. Label your quilt.

### Quilting Suggestion
*Outline-quilt the appliqués and quilt in-the-ditch along the background seams. Quilt waves in the lattice below the lighthouse and light beams radiating from the lighthouse.*

# LUNCH TIME

**Finished size: 35" x 47"**

The pelican is one of the most photographed and painted shore birds. He certainly had to appear in this book. The sandpipers, or sanderlings, marching down and across the borders on their way to lunch make this quilt even more reminiscent of the Florida shore.

## MATERIALS: 42"-WIDE FABRIC

¾ yd. for background
¼ yd. for inner border
1 yd. for outer border
⅓ yd. for sand
¼ yd. for pelican body
¼ yd. for sandpiper bodies
⅓ yd. for pilings
¼ yd. for pelican back and lower tail
¼ yd. for pelican wing
⅛ yd. for sandpiper caps
⅛ yd. for sandpiper wings
½ yd. for binding
1⅔ yds. for backing
Scraps for under-wing, beak, feet, fish,
    and piling tops
40" x 52" piece of thin batting
Gold and black embroidery floss

## CUTTING

**From the background fabric, cut:**
1 piece, 24" x 36"

**From the fabric for the inner border, cut:**
2 strips, each 1½" x 24½"
2 strips, each 1½" x 34½"

**From the fabric for the outer border, cut:**
2 strips, each 6½" x 36½"
2 strips, each 6½" x 37½"

**From the sand fabric, cut:**
1 rectangle, 12" x 24"
1 rectangle, 6" x 20"

## APPLIQUÉING THE QUILT TOP

Make templates for all the appliqué pieces, using the patterns on the pullout and on page 50. Refer to "Preassembled Appliqué" on pages 6–7. Using appropriate fabrics, prepare and appliqué the pieces as follows.

1. Using Preassembled-Appliqué Technique 2, appliqué middle beak 8, then fish 7 and upper beak 9 to lower beak 6.

2. Using Preassembled-Appliqué Technique 2, appliqué body 1 to under-wing 2, wing 4 to tail 5, and then back 3. Appliqué the beak and the feet to the body.

3. Using Preassembled-Appliqué Technique 1, appliqué piling tops to pilings.

4. Referring to the quilt diagram, draw a gentle curve across the 12" x 24" sand rectangle. Add a ¼"-wide seam allowance and cut the excess fabric away. Draw another gentle curve on the remaining 6" x 20" sand piece, add a ¼"-wide seam allowance, and trim the excess fabric.

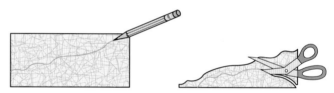

5. Appliqué the piling 1 unit to the 24" x 36" background piece, and then appliqué the large sand piece, covering the bottom of the piling.

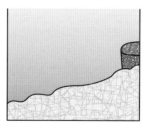 

6. Appliqué the piling 2 unit onto the sand, approximately 4½" from the right seam line. Appliqué the small sand piece, partially covering the bottom of piling 2.

7. Appliqué the pelican to the top of piling 2, starting with the back foot, then the body unit and the front foot.
8. Stitch the eye with the stem and satin stitch. Add details to the head and beak with the stem stitch.
9. Trim the Pelican block to 22½" x 34½".

## ADDING BORDERS

1. Sew the 1½" x 34½" inner-border strips to the sides of the Pelican block; then sew the 1½" x 24½" strips to the top and bottom.
2. Prepare the appliqué pieces for the 9 sandpipers, using the templates on the pullout. Using Preassembled-Appliqué Technique 1, appliqué the cap and wings to the body. Cut out the sandpipers, adding a ⅛"-wide seam allowance.
3. For the appliquéd side border, position 5 sandpipers on a 6½" x 37½" outer-border strip, spacing them evenly. Appliqué in place.

4. For the bottom border, position 4 sandpipers on a 6½" x 36½" outer-border strip, spacing them evenly. Appliqué the sandpipers in place.
5. Using the templates on the pullout, trace the sandpiper beaks and legs. Embroider the beaks and legs with a satin stitch. Make French knots for the eyes.
6. Trim both side border strips to 6" x 36½".
7. Trim top and bottom border strips to 6" x 35½".
8. Sew the outer borders to the sides of the quilt top, then to the top and bottom.

## FINISHING

1. Layer the quilt top with batting and backing.
2. Baste, and then quilt as desired.
3. Label your quilt.

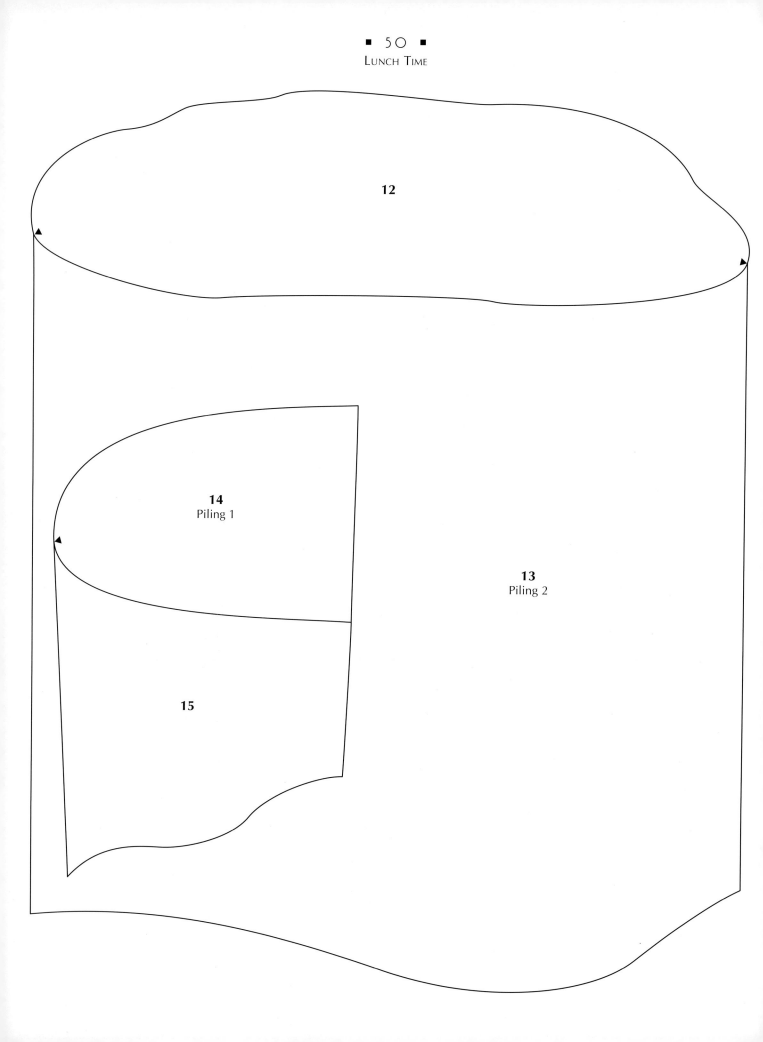

**12**

**14**
Piling 1

**13**
Piling 2

**15**

# A FLORIDA DREAM

**Quilt Size: 37" x 31"**

This whimsical wall hanging is fun to make even
if you aren't a Floridian. The thought of standing in
a beautiful ocean with a cheery little quilt, holding
winning lottery tickets, could be anyone's dream.

## MATERIALS: 42"-WIDE FABRIC

½ yd. light blue for sky
⅞ yd. medium blue for flamingo background
¼ yd. medium pink for flamingo wing and
    neck
¼ yd. dark pink for flamingo body and legs
Fat quarter for miniquilt border
¼ yd. for palm leaves
Scraps for tree trunk, flowers, water, sand,
    boat, sails, sun, beak, miniquilt corners,
    and lottery ticket
¼ yd. black-and-white check for first border
¼ yd. for second border
½ yd. for third border
1¼ yds. for backing
⅓ yd. for binding
35" x 41" piece of thin batting
Permanent marking pen
Gold embroidery floss

## CUTTING

**From the light blue, cut:**
1 square, 12" x 12"

**From the medium blue, cut:**
1 piece, 24" x 34"

**From the fabric for the first border, cut:**
2 strips, each 1½" x 32½"
2 strips, each 1½" x 24½"

**From the fabric for the second border, cut:**
2 strips, each 2½" x 34½"
2 strips, each 2½" x 28½"

**From the fabric for the third border, cut:**
2 strips, each 4½" x 38½"
2 strips, each 4½" x 36½"

## APPLIQUÉING THE QUILT TOP

Make templates for all the appliqué pieces, using the patterns on the pullout. Refer to "Preassembled Appliqué" on pages 6–7; use Technique 2 for steps 1–5. Cut appliqué pieces from the appropriate fabrics and appliqué as follows.

1. Appliqué the flower petals to each other in numerical order. Using the stem stitch and French knot, embroider the flower centers.
2. Appliqué the pieces in the following order:
    Boat to sky—align the raw edge of the
        boat hull with the lower edge of the
        sky piece
    Water to sky
    Tree trunk, then leaves in numerical order
    Sand to water
    Sun to sky
    Flower unit to sand
3. Trace the complete miniquilt border onto a large piece of freezer paper. Press the freezer paper onto the border fabric, draw around it, and cut out the border piece, adding a ⅛"-wide seam allowance. Position the border on top of the appliquéd scene. Pin it in place and appliqué the inner edge of the oval.
4. Remove the freezer paper and appliqué the top corner pieces to the border.
5. Using Preassembled-Appliqué Technique 2, appliqué the flamingo wings to each other in numerical order.
6. Appliqué the lottery tickets to the lower body, and then add the wing unit.
7. Appliqué the upper beak to the neck. Add the eye.
8. Appliqué the legs and flamingo body to the 24" x 34" blue background piece.
9. Pin the remaining pieces in position and appliqué, beginning with the lower beak. Appliqué the miniquilt to the background, and then add the flamingo neck unit, overlapping the miniquilt with the upper beak.
10. Cut away the background fabric behind the flamingo body and the miniquilt.
11. Write or embroider the word "lottery" on one ticket and a special number on the second ticket.

## Adding the Borders

Depending on the scale of your checked fabric, you may want to vary the measurements of the quilt top and borders. I mitered the outer border of my quilt to make stripes meet. Refer to "Borders with Mitered Corners" on page 9.

1. Trim the quilt top to measure 22½" x 32½".
2. Sew the 1½" x 32½" first-border strips to the sides of the wall hanging, and then sew the 1½" x 24½" strips to the top and bottom.
3. Sew the 2½" x 34½" second-border strips to the sides of the quilt top and the 2½" x 28½" strips to the top and bottom.
4. Sew the 4½" x 38½" third-border strips to the sides of the quilt top and the 4½" x 36½" strips to the top and bottom.

## Finishing

1. Layer the quilt top with batting and backing.
2. Baste, and then quilt as desired.
3. Label your quilt.

### Quilting Suggestion

*Outline-quilt all the appliqué motifs. Quilt ripples and circles around the flamingo legs and throughout the rest of the background. Crosshatch the background of the miniquilt.*

# IN MY LADY'S GARDEN

**Finished size: 46" x 64"**

I designed this quilt after several trips to New Orleans,
a city of many wrought-iron fences and beautiful flowers.
I hope this project will not only put you in the mood to
make a quilt, but also to take a trip to the "Big Easy."

# MATERIALS: 42"-WIDE FABRIC

4 yds. black for background, wrought iron
  fence, border and binding
1 yd. white for picket fence
⅔ yd. green for stems
1½ yds. dark red for border
  (1¼ yds. if pieced)
¼ yd. *each* of 5 reds (light to medium)
*Optional:* scraps of 5 additional reds
⅛ yd. red for buds
⅓ yd. green for leaves, buds, and flower bases
⅛ yd. *each* of 4 shades of hot pink for circles
2 yds. for backing
49" x 68" piece of thin batting
Black embroidery floss
¼"-wide and ⅜"-wide bias bars

# CUTTING

**From the lengthwise grain of the black, cut:**
2 strips, each 2½" x 70"
2 strips, each 2½" x 46½"
2 strips, each 2½" x 50"
2 strips, each 2½" x 26½"
4 pieces, each 2½" x 22½"
4 pieces, each 10½" x 18"
13 strips, each 1" x 80"
90 fence hearts

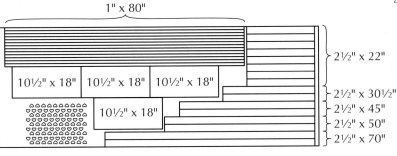

# From the white, cut:
3 pieces, each 2½" x 18"
3 pieces, each 10½" x 22"
2 pieces, each 4½" x 22"

### From the green for stems, cut:
2 bias strips, each 1" x 20"
6 to 10 bias strips, each 1½" wide,
totaling approximately 105" in length

### From the lengthwise grain of the dark red, cut:
2 strips, each 6½" x 66"
2 strips, each 6½" x 46"

# PIECING THE BACKGROUND

1. Sew 22½"-long black and white strips together to
   make 2 strip sets as shown.
2. Crosscut the sets into 2½"-wide strips, 7 strips of
   Row 1 and 6 strips of Row 2.

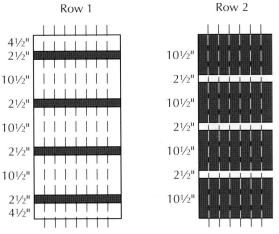

Crosscut every 2½" for 7 strips of Row 1
and 6 strips of Row 2.

3. Sew the strips together lengthwise, alternating Rows 1 and 2 to create the white picket-fence background.

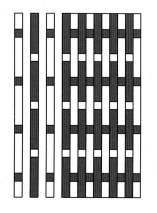

4. Sew the 2½" x 46½" black strips to the sides of the quilt top; sew the 2½" x 26½" strips to the top and bottom.

## APPLIQUÉING THE FLOWERS

Make templates for all the appliqué pieces, using the patterns on the pullout and on pages 58–62. Refer to "Preassembled Appliqué" on pages 6–7. Cut flowers 1–9 from the appropriate fabrics, using Technique 2 to make the flowers.

1. Appliqué the flower pieces to each other in numerical order. Embroider the stamens with a stem stitch and a French knot.

2. Using the red fabric, make folded rose buds as shown. Appliqué the bud covers to the buds.

3. Fold each 1½"-wide green bias strip in half lengthwise, wrong sides together. Stitch along the long raw edge, using a ¼"-wide seam allowance. Insert the ⅜" bias bar into each tube, center the seam allowance on the back, and press. Cut the bias tubes into the desired lengths for stems.

4. Arrange the stems, leaves, and flowers on the quilt top. Pin or baste the pieces in place. Appliqué the stems, leaves, buds, and then the flower units to the background.

## ADDING THE BORDERS

1. Fold each black 1"-wide strip in half lengthwise, wrong sides together. Stitch along the long raw edge, using a ¼"-wide seam allowance.

2. Slide a ¼" bias bar into each tube, center the seam allowance on the back, and press. Continue sliding the bar down the length of the tube until you have pressed the entire length. Trim the seam allowance if necessary.

3. Mark 2 lines on each red border strip, one line 2⅛" from the inner edge, the other line 4½" from the inner edge.

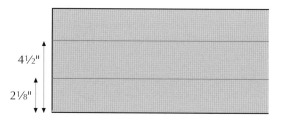

4. Pin a pressed black tube over each of the 2 lengthwise lines on each border strip and appliqué.

5. Cut the remaining tubes into 90 segments, each 6½" long, for the fence posts. To mark the placement of the "wrought-iron" fence posts, find the centers of the 6½" x 46" red strips. Measure ⅞" from the center on each side and make a mark in the inner and outer seam allowance. Draw a line across the strip to connect the marks. Measure 1¾" from these lines and make another set of marks. Draw a line connecting them. Continue marking at 1¾" intervals until you have 8 fence-post lines on each side of the center.

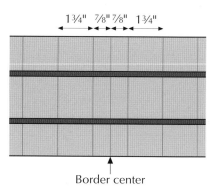

Border center

■ 57 ■

6. Find the center of each 6½" x 66½" red strip and draw a line from one seam allowance to the other. From the center line, measure outward on each side in scant 1¾" increments, marking in the inner and outer seam allowances. Connect the marks with a line across the border strip. Continue until you have marked 14 increments on each side of the center.
7. Center a 6½"-long black fence post over each post line and appliqué.
8. Sew the 2½" x 45" black strips to the appliquéd border strips, matching the centers of the strips. Sew the 2½" x 70" black strips to the 6½" x 66" appliquéd border strips, matching the centers of the strips.
9. Appliqué a heart to the top of each fence post, placing the tip of each heart just at the seam line of the outer border.

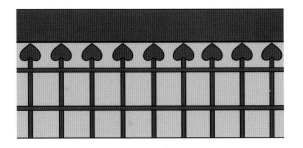

10. Referring to "Borders with Mitered Corners" on page 9, sew the border strips to the quilt top and miter the corners.
11. Cut 4 pieces of the black tube, each 7" long, and appliqué one over the mitered seam at each corner, hiding the joins of the horizontal bars.

## ADDING THE DETAILS

1. Appliqué 3 black heart outlines in each corner as shown in the quilt diagram. Appliqué the inner edges first.
2. Trace the small, medium, and large circles on the pullout onto heat-resistant template material.
3. Trace the circles onto the pink and red fabrics and cut them out, adding ¼"-wide seam allowances.
4. Without knotting the thread, stitch around each circle in the seam allowance to gather. Put the template on the wrong side of the circle. Gather the seam allowance up around the template and press.
5. Loosen the gathering stitch, remove the template, regather carefully, and knot the thread.
6. Appliqué the circles in place using the photograph on page 21 as a guide. Appliqué the small leaves that overlap the borders.

## FINISHING

1. Layer the quilt top with batting and backing.
2. Baste, and then quilt as desired.
3. Label your quilt.

### Quilting Suggestion
*Outline-quilt each of the appliqué motifs in the center and borders. Fill the center background with clamshells. Quilt two parallel lines in the outer border.*

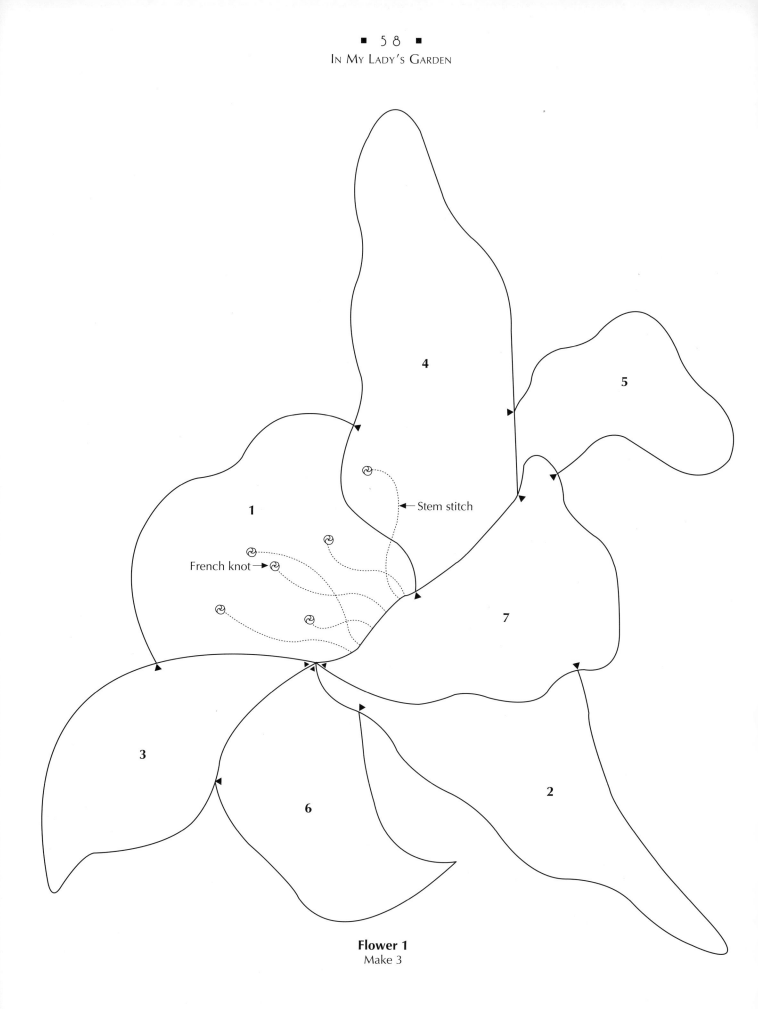

**Flower 1**
Make 3

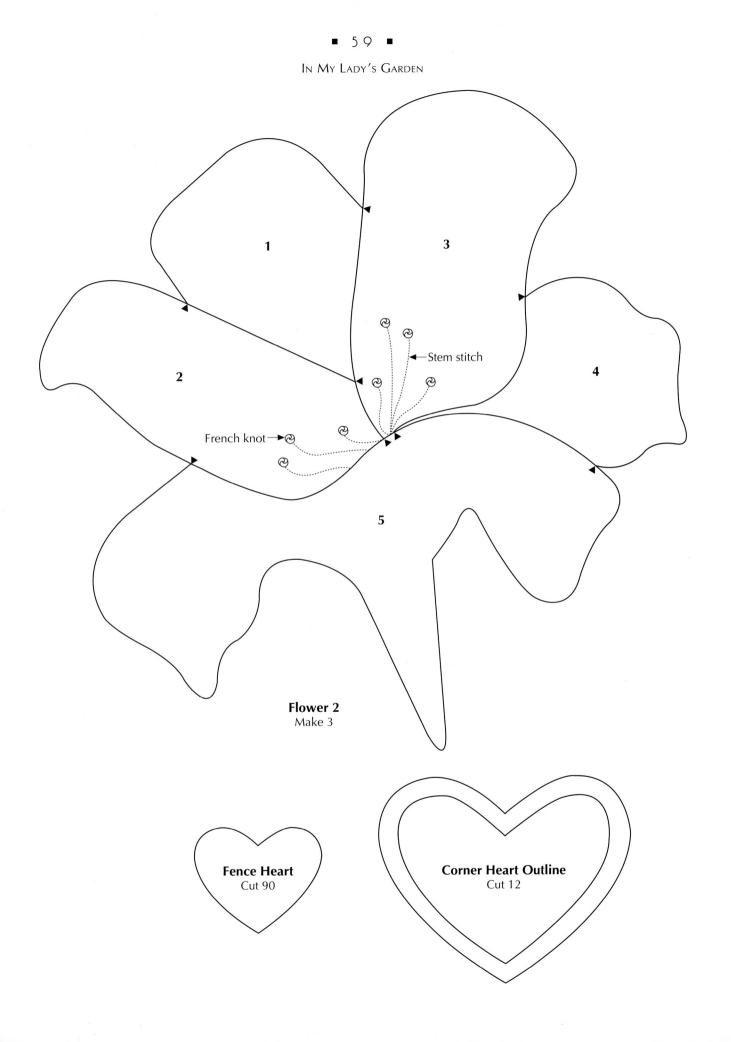

1

3

2

Stem stitch

4

French knot

5

**Flower 2**
Make 3

**Fence Heart**
Cut 90

**Corner Heart Outline**
Cut 12

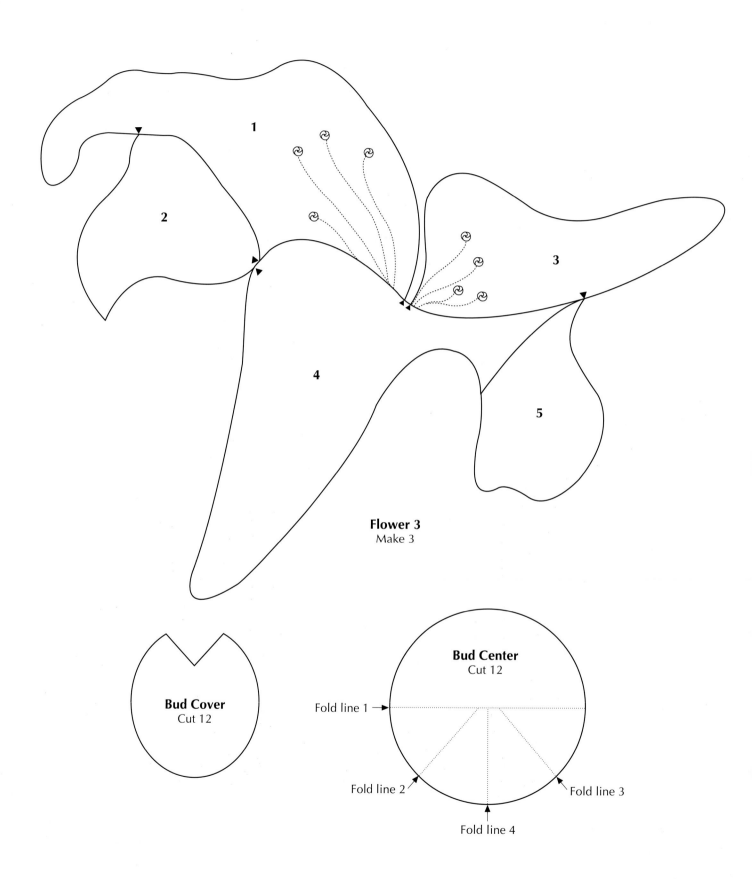

**Flower 3**
Make 3

**Bud Cover**
Cut 12

**Bud Center**
Cut 12

Fold line 1

Fold line 2

Fold line 3

Fold line 4

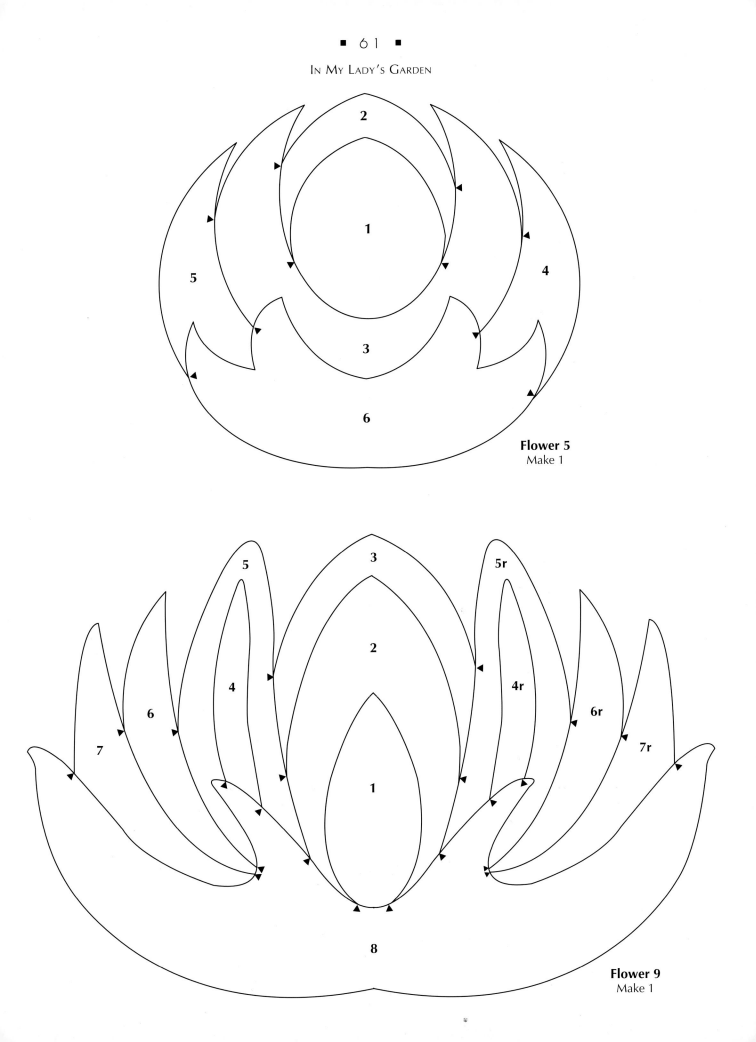

**Flower 5**
Make 1

**Flower 9**
Make 1

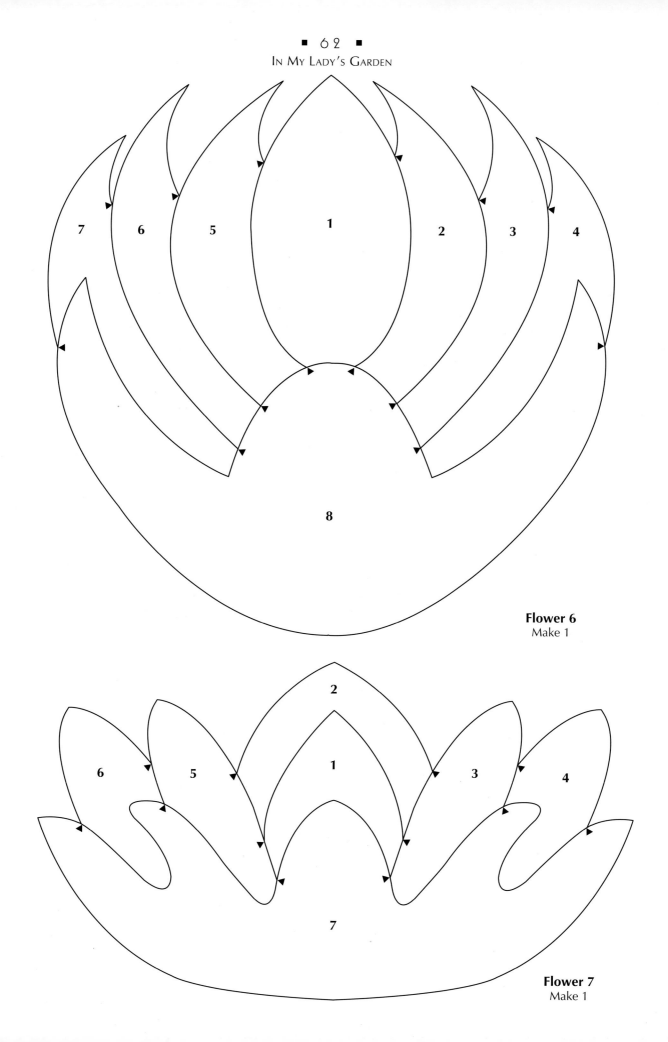

**Flower 6**
Make 1

**Flower 7**
Make 1

# ᴛHE ᴍARKETPLACE

**Finished size: 63" x 40"**

When I opened my quilt shop, I listed several possible names
and sketched a logo for each. With a little help from my friends,
my Quilters Marketplace sketch became a refined drawing, and a
logo was launched. Here is that sketch turned into a quilt pattern,
something to embellish with lots of silk-ribbon flowers.

## MATERIALS: 42"-WIDE FABRIC

½ yd. blue for sky
1 fat quarter *each* of brown, yellow, gray, and
   pink for buildings
⅛ yd. for sidewalk
⅓ yd. yellow for first border
½ yd. pink for pieced second border (1⅓ yds.
   if not pieced)
½ yd. green for pieced third border (1½ yds.
   if not pieced)
1⅔ yds. large-scale floral for fourth border
¼ yd. for tree trunk
¼ yd. for palm fronds
⅛ yd. dark brown for roof
Scraps for appliqué
Embroidery floss in copper, brown, black, and
   2 or 3 shades each of green and gold
4mm, 7mm, and 13mm silk ribbon in assorted
   colors
2 yds. for backing
44" x 67" piece of thin batting
½ yd. for binding
Chenille and embroidery needles

## CUTTING

**From the blue, cut:**
1 piece, 16½" x 42"

**From the fat quarters, cut:**
1 square, 10½" x 10½", for building A
1 piece, 6½" x 10½", for building B
1 piece, 6½" x 13¾", for building C
1 piece, 7" x 10½", for building D

**From the fabric for the sidewalk, cut:**
1 piece, 4½" x 41"

**From the fabric for the first border, cut:**
2 strips, each 2½" x 41½"
2 strips, each 2½" x 21"

**From the fabric for the second border, cut:**
3 strips, each 3½" x 42". Cut 1 strip in half lengthwise; then sew 1 half-strip to each full-length strip.
Trim each pieced strip to 45½" long.
2 strips, each 3½" x 25"

**From the fabric for the third border, cut:**
3 strips, each 1¾" x 42". Cut 1 strip in half lengthwise; then sew 1 half-strip to each full-length strip.
Trim each pieced strip to 51½" long.
2 strips, each 1¾" x 27"

**From the fabric for the fourth border, cut:**
3 strips, each 6½" x 56½". Cut 1 strip in half lengthwise; then sew 1 half-strip to each full-length strip.
Trim each pieced strip to 56½" long.
3 strips, each 6½" x 49". Cut 1 strip in half lengthwise; then sew 1 half-strip to each full-length strip.
Trim each pieced strip to 49" long.

## APPLIQUÉING THE QUILT TOP

Make templates for all the appliqué pieces, using
the patterns on the pullout and on pages 66–70. Refer
to "Preassembled Appliqué" on pages 6–7. Prepare
and appliqué the pieces as follows.

1. Use Preassembled-Appliqué Technique 2 to
   appliqué the fronds of the palm trees to each
   other in numerical order. (For variety, you can
   make 1 or more of the trees using the palm tree
   from "A Florida Dream" on the pullout.)
2. Place 2 tree tops on the background so that they
   will lie behind the buildings and appliqué.
3. Using Preassembled-Appliqué Technique 1,
   appliqué the windows, door, and awnings to each
   building. Appliqué the shutters to buildings B and
   C, and the steps to building D.
4. Using Preassembled-Appliqué Technique 1,
   appliqué the roofs to buildings A, C, and D.
   Appliqué the completed buildings to the sky
   background, aligning the bottom edge of each
   with the bottom edge of the sky. Cut away the sky
   fabric behind each building.
5. Sew the sidewalk to the bottom edge of the sky-
   building unit using a ¼"-wide seam allowance.
6. Using Preassembled-Appliqué Technique 2,
   appliqué the lamppost pieces to each other in
   numerical order. Pin the unit in place on the
   background and appliqué.
7. Using Preassembled-Appliqué Technique 2,
   appliqué the wheelbarrow pieces to each other in
   numerical order. Pin the unit in place on the
   background and appliqué. Appliqué the flower
   pots and the steps of the pink building to the
   background.

8. Embroider the window and door details.
9. Trim the background to 17" x 41½".

## ADDING THE BORDERS

1. Sew the 2½" x 41½" first-border strips to the top and bottom of the quilt top, and the 2½" x 21" strips to the sides.
2. Sew the 3½" x 45½" second-border strips to the top and bottom of the quilt top and the 3½" x 27" strips to the sides.
3. Sew the 1¾" x 51½" third-border strips to the top and bottom of the quilt top and the 1¾" x 29" strips to the sides.
4. Sew the 6½" x 54" fourth-border strips to the top and bottom of the quilt top and the 6½" x 41½" strips to the sides.
5. Appliqué the remaining tree trunks and frond units in place, overlapping the borders as shown in the quilt plan. Using the stem stitch, embroider veins on the fronds.

6. Embroider silk-ribbon flowers in the pots, flower boxes, and wheelbarrow and around the buildings. See the examples below for inspiration.

## FINISHING

1. Layer the quilt top with batting and backing.
2. Baste, and then quilt as desired.
3. Label your quilt.

### Quilting Suggestion

*Outline-quilt each appliqué unit and the flowers in the fourth-border print. Quilt the other borders in-the-ditch. Use special care as you quilt around the silk-ribbon embroidery.*

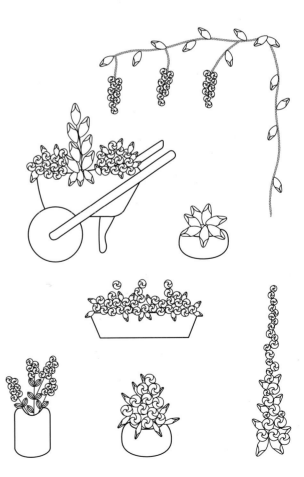

| | | | |
|---|---|---|---|
| ≋≋ | Stem stitch | ⬯ | Ribbon stitch |
| ☺ | French knot | — | Straight stitch |
| ⬯ | Lazy daisy stitch | | |

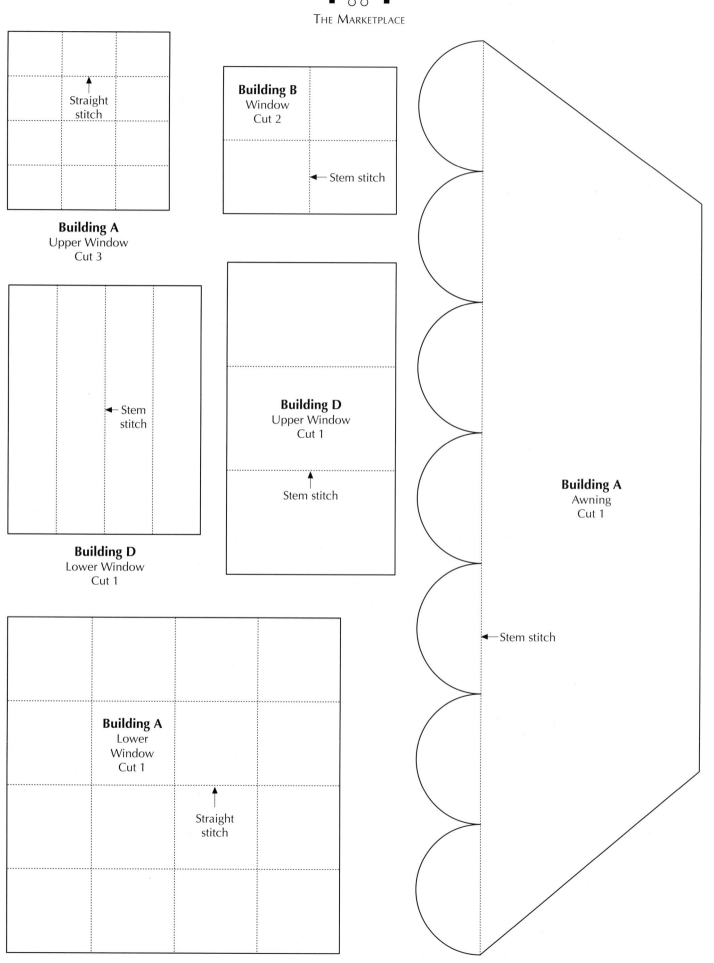

**Building A**
Upper Window
Cut 3

Straight stitch

**Building B**
Window
Cut 2

Stem stitch

**Building D**
Lower Window
Cut 1

Stem stitch

**Building D**
Upper Window
Cut 1

Stem stitch

**Building A**
Lower Window
Cut 1

Straight stitch

**Building A**
Awning
Cut 1

Stem stitch

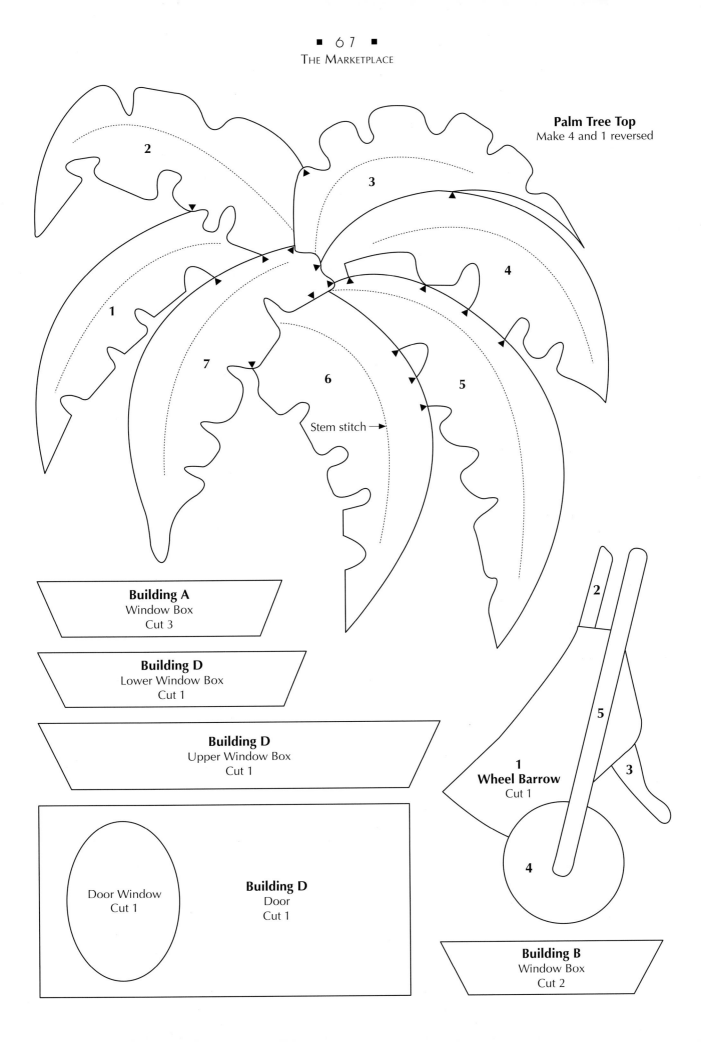

**Palm Tree Top**
Make 4 and 1 reversed

2

3

1

4

7

6

5

Stem stitch →

**Building A**
Window Box
Cut 3

**Building D**
Lower Window Box
Cut 1

**Building D**
Upper Window Box
Cut 1

Door Window
Cut 1

**Building D**
Door
Cut 1

2

5

1
**Wheel Barrow**
Cut 1

3

4

**Building B**
Window Box
Cut 2

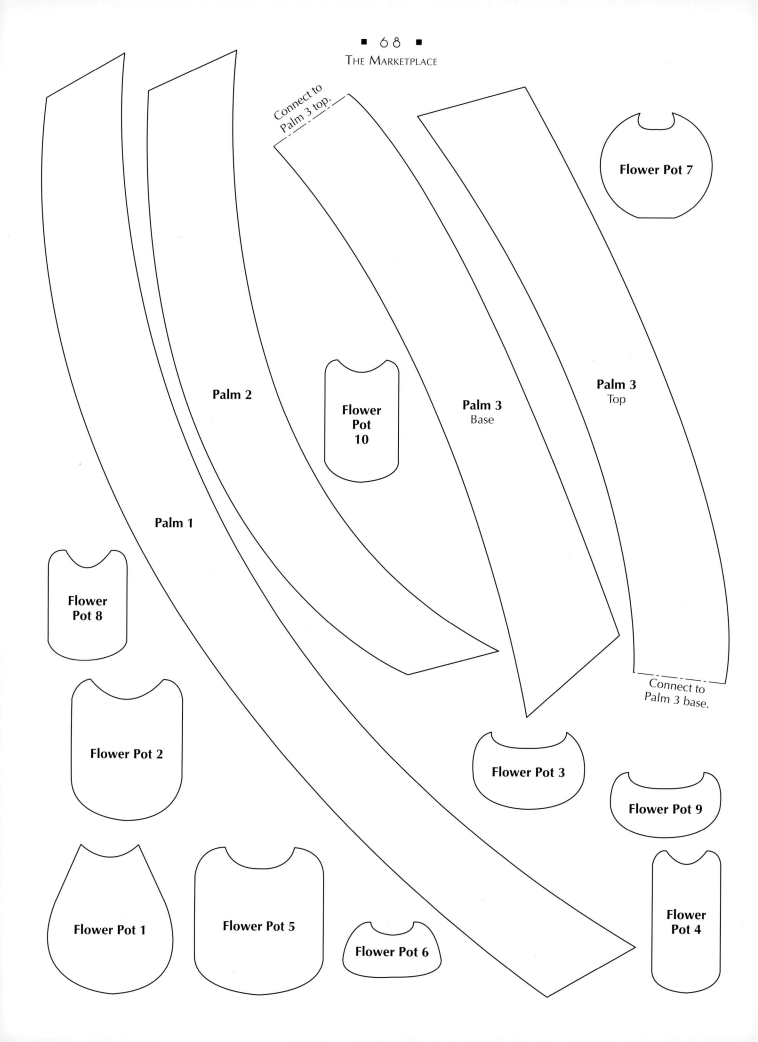

Connect to Palm 3 top.

Flower Pot 7

Palm 2

Flower Pot 10

Palm 3 Base

Palm 3 Top

Palm 1

Flower Pot 8

Connect to Palm 3 base.

Flower Pot 2

Flower Pot 3

Flower Pot 9

Flower Pot 1

Flower Pot 5

Flower Pot 6

Flower Pot 4

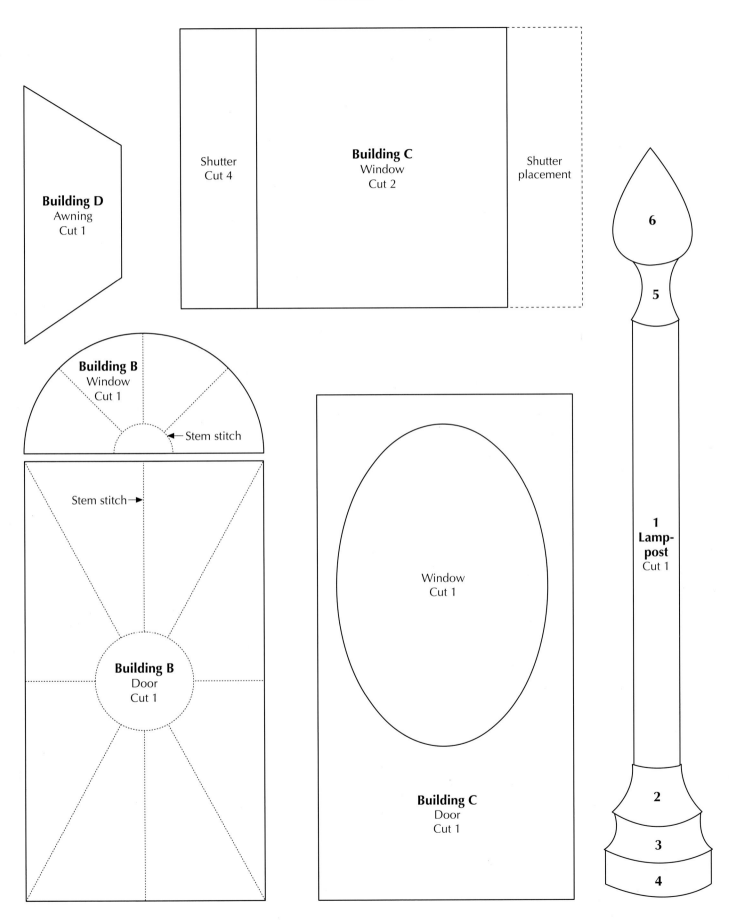

Building D
Awning
Cut 1

Shutter
Cut 4

**Building C**
Window
Cut 2

Shutter
placement

**6**

**5**

**Building B**
Window
Cut 1

← Stem stitch

Stem stitch →

**1**
**Lamp-post**
Cut 1

Window
Cut 1

**Building B**
Door
Cut 1

**2**

**3**

**4**

**Building C**
Door
Cut 1

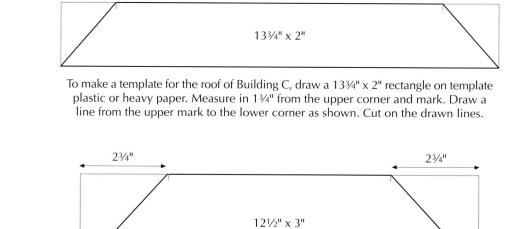

1¾"    13¾" x 2"    1¾"

To make a template for the roof of Building C, draw a 13¾" x 2" rectangle on template plastic or heavy paper. Measure in 1¾" from the upper corner and mark. Draw a line from the upper mark to the lower corner as shown. Cut on the drawn lines.

2¾"    12½" x 3"    2¾"

To make a template for the roof of Building A, draw a 12½" x 3" rectangle on template plastic or heavy paper. Measure in 2¾" from the upper corner and mark. Draw a line from the upper mark to the lower corner as shown. Cut on the drawn lines.

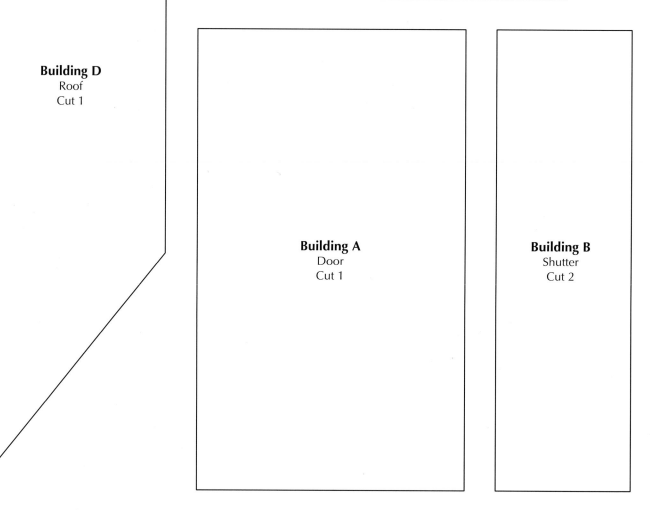

**Building D**
Step
Cut 2

**Building D**
Roof
Cut 1

**Building A**
Door
Cut 1

**Building B**
Shutter
Cut 2

# MEET THE AUTHOR

My quilting life began in 1976. As Americans were celebrating their nation's birthday, sewers were celebrating a rebirth of quiltmaking. My historical-society friends and I put together a wonderful quilt depicting the history of our community. That quilt still hangs in the city hall of Bridgeton, Missouri.

I went on to make family quilts with the help of my "quilting" grandmother. She made whole-cloth quilts perfectly and often. It looked so easy; I didn't understand at the time how difficult it was. Now I realize how much I missed by not having her teach me more about her wonderful craft.

I made baby quilts without benefit of quilt shops, books, or television shows. I made them by drawing designs on fabric, then appliquéing the designs onto

backgrounds. I moved on to making quilted game boards for games such as Candyland, Monopoly, and backgammon.

In 1986 I decided to make a quilt for the Great American Quilt Contest. Imagine my surprise when I received the call informing me that I had won for the state of Florida (see page 4). Off to the show we went—what fun it was to meet the other winners.

Soon after the contest, I opened Quilters Marketplace in Delray Beach, Florida, where I continue to teach appliqué, my technique of choice. I prefer to re-create appliquéd pictures rather than piece them. I share my love of the art of quilting by lecturing, teaching guild classes, judging quilt shows, and making quilts.

# Publications and Products

Many titles are available at your local quilt shop.
For more information, write for a free color catalog
to That Patchwork Place, Inc., PO Box 118, Bothell,
WA 98041-0118 USA.

☎ U.S. and Canada, call **1-800-426-3126** for the
name and location of the quilt shop nearest you.
**Int'l:** 1-425-483-3313    **Fax:** 1-425-486-7596
**E-mail:** info@patchwork.com
**Web:** www.patchwork.com                    8.97